The Hollywood Musical

Second Edition

D0265610

British Film Institute Cinema Series

Edited by Ed Buscombe

The British Film Institute Cinema Series opens up a new area of cinema publishing with books that will appeal to people who are already interested in the cinema but want to know more, written in an accessible style by authors who have some authority in their field. The authors write about areas of the cinema where there is substantial popular interest, but as yet little serious writing, or they bring together for a wider audience some of the important ideas which have been developed in film studies in recent years.

<table>
<tr><td>Richard Dyer:</td><td>Heavenly Bodies: Film Stars and Society</td></tr>
<tr><td>Thomas Elsaesser:</td><td>New German Cinema: A History</td></tr>
<tr><td>Jane Feuer:</td><td>The Hollywood Musical (2nd Edition)</td></tr>
<tr><td>Lucy Fischer:</td><td>Shot/Countershot: Film Tradition and Women's Film</td></tr>
<tr><td>Jill Forbes:</td><td>The Cinema in France</td></tr>
<tr><td>Steve Neale:</td><td>Cinema and Technology</td></tr>
</table>

Series Standing Order

If you would like to receive future titles in this series as they are published, you can make use of our standing order facility. To place a standing order please contact your bookseller or, in case of difficulty, write to us at the address below with your name and address and the name of the series. Please state with which title you wish to begin your standing order.
(If you live outside the United Kingdom we may not have the rights for your area, in which case we will forward your order to the publisher concerned.)

Customer Services Department, Macmillan Distribution Ltd
Houndmills, Basingstoke, Hampshire, RG21 2XS, England.

Jane Feuer

THE HOLLYWOOD MUSICAL

Second Edition

M

First edition 1982
Second edition 1993

Published by
THE MACMILLAN PRESS LTD
Houndmills, Basingstoke, Hampshire RG21 2XS
and London
Companies and representatives
throughout the world

ISBN 0–333–58341–8 (hardcover)
ISBN 0–333–58342–6 (paperback)

A catalogue record for this book is available
from the British Library.

Printed in Hong Kong

To my grandfather, Joseph Rodner

Contents

Preface to the First Edition

Twenty-five years ago most film buffs would have scoffed at the idea that serious books could be written about John Wayne bang-bang Westerns and Rock Hudson kiss-kiss weepies. It was only when Hollywood genre films began to be seen from the perspective of their ideological and cultural meanings (rather than as star vehicles or 'pure entertainment') that Westerns, melodramas and *films noirs* became accessible to critical inquiry. Yet the genre most of us think of as quintessentially Hollywood was the only one not fertilized by the new interest in film as ideology. Westerns might now be seen as a conflict between chaos and civilization, but Fred Astaire remained ineffable.

We need a key to open the shimmering glass door musicals place between themselves and any form of intellectual inquiry. Musicals seem particularly resistant to analysis; peel away the tinsel and you find the real tinsel underneath. Musicals epitomize the golden age of Hollywood's studio era in the popular imagination, as the nostalgia films **That's Entertainment I** and **II** make clear (the French titles, **Il était une fois à Hollywood** and **Hollywood... Hollywood!**, make an even closer connection).

The musical is Hollywood writ large. Once we see it this way, the door swings open. For musicals, in being about Hollywood, are also about themselves. The 'golden years' of Hollywood musicals spanned the studio era from the coming of sound in 1927 to the television era of the mid-1950s. **The Jazz Singer** in 1927 followed a show-business plot, and during the talkie boom that followed from 1929 to 1933 a large percentage of early musicals took for their subjects the world of entertainment: Broadway, vaudeville, the Ziegfeld Follies, burlesque, night clubs, the circus, Tin Pan Alley and, to a lesser extent, mass entertainment media in the form of radio or the movies themselves. 'Putting on a show' was a formula that made breaking into song and dance plausible, thereby justifying the inclusion of musical numbers in a film. Such a trend continued with **All That Jazz** (1970) portraying the crisis of a middle-aged director of Broadway musicals and movies, and **Fame** (1980) continuing the Rooney–Garland tradition of kids trying to break into show business. I hope to argue that not only backstage musicals, but others as well, in being about entertainment, are also about themselves.

This most seemingly anti-intellectual of genres thus carries its own 'ideological project'. Musicals not only gave the most intense (because the least intellectualized) pleasure to their audience but also supplied a justification for that pleasure. Musicals not only *showed* you singing and dancing; they were *about* singing and dancing, about the nature and importance of that experience. Once we have found the solution to the problems musicals pose for the critic in this concept of auto-apology, certain films appear blatantly obvious in this mission. Take, for example, two 1956 Fred Astaire vehicles, **Funny Face** and **Silk Stockings**. The former poses the question: can a girl give up the life of an existentialist bookworm in order to be loved by Fred Astaire and transformed into an artificial photographic image of unutterable mystery and beauty? The latter has a Soviet Cyd Charisse inquiring of international capitalist Astaire, does every girl you kiss change her politics? The answer in both cases is yes, and I have heard the right answer out of the mouths (unconsciously or not!) even of left-wing feminists.

Theories of counter-cinema based purely on abstraction and cognition fail to take adequate account of the power of dominant cinema's appeal to the emotions, an appeal that addresses itself in a systematic manner to basic human needs, albeit in a way which affirms the cultural status quo and forecloses change. But it is not only through the intensity of its appeal to the emotions (fantasies of love, harmony, spontaneity, etc.) that the musical mounts a challenge to modernism. We like to think that the difference betweeen classical Hollywood narratives and deconstructive modernist films is that the former are totally oblivious of their own status as created artifact and as cultural sign. Yet within its texts the musical makes use of a repertory of techniques usually associated with modernist art. No longer can modernism be defined as a set of formal devices that Godard uses but Charles Walters doesn't. Like Cubist paintings, musicals fragment space, multiplying and dividing the human figure into splits, doubles, alter egos. Like post-modern dance, musicals place a premium on an impression of spontaneity, group choreography and a naturalization of technique. Like Godard, musicals employ direct address, multiple and divided characters. Like Fellini, musicals insist on multiple levels of reality and on the continuity between dream images and waking life. Yet the Hollywood musical resembles none of these modernist works. Formally bold, it is culturally the most conservative of genres. In the pages which follow I will attempt to untangle this seeming paradox.

Preface to the Second Edition

If the traditional Hollywood musical seemed an archaic art form in 1982 when this book was first published, by 1992 it appeared positively moribund. Although many of the films persisted as 'classics' to be taught in film courses or as 'nostalgia films' to fill the endless broadcast hours on TNT and American Movie Classics cable channels, the genre as a forum for exploring our current concerns or as a display case for the best of contemporary entertainment practices certainly seemed to have peaked in the 1950s and then died rapidly with the end of the studio era. Since the mid-1950s rock and pop have been the dominant forms of popular music and these forms appeared more suited to audio and concert presentational formats than to the movie musical with its double requirement of numbers *and* narrative. Only a few adaptations of Broadway shows (e.g. **A Chorus Line**) and a few nostalgia films and 'arty' musicals (**New York, New York** is both) persisted into the 1970s and 1980s. Both the narrative type of music and the naive optimism and gender politics of Hollywood musicals appeared obsolete in post-1960s America. Thus I was able to argue in the 1982 version of this book that the artifacts keeping old Hollywood musicals alive were no longer Hollywood musicals themselves.

In 1992 this is both more true and less true, depending upon how one conceptualizes MTV and the rebirth of the teenpic/teen musical that has accompanied the music video. My desire to do a second edition of this book that tried to account for this new kind of musical came about because I was struck by the intensity of pleasure I felt viewing **Flashdance**, **Dirty Dancing** and **Hairspray**. It was almost like the feeling that kept me going back for more to old MGM musicals, and quite unlike the intellectual pleasure I received from deconstructive works such as **Pennies from Heaven**. The additional material on the 1980s teen musical is in part an attempt to theorize this pleasure.

In 1982 mine was one of a handful of academic studies of film musicals. Since then many articles and a number of books have been published (referenced in the Notes to the Postscript), most notably Rick Altman's 1987 opus *The American Film Musical*, the definitive work on the subject and one that had in manuscript heavily influenced my own thinking on the subject. My disagreements with Altman's book thus coincided with dissatisfaction at what I'd omitted from my own book: any consideration of the sexual and gender politics of musicals beyond saying that they reinforce heterosexuality (a truism if ever there was one), an inability to account for the actual historical audiences for musicals beyond paying lip-service to the idea of an 'interpretive community', and a theory of genre based on a classical period framed on either side by experimentation and deconstruction. The additional material in this edition is also an attempt to correct some of these omissions. The last section in particular is a quite preliminary bid to include musicals in the emergent field of Gay Studies as it develops across disciplines and calls into question many of our received beliefs about almost everything, not the least being the heterosexuality of musicals.

List of Illustrations

Acknowledgements

This project began as a paper for a graduate seminar on popular narratives at the University of Iowa in 1975. It grew into a dissertation and, now, a book. Without the aid and collaboration of the teacher of that seminar, Charles F. 'Rick' Altman, it might have remained an embryo.

Thomas Elsaesser, Jim Collins, Pam Falkenberg and Alan Williams contributed to my thinking about musicals, as they read the manuscript at various stages. Thomas Schatz, in addition, made numerous suggestions for 'de-dissertating' it.

I must thank my own Maxwell Perkins, Ed Buscombe, for subtle but forceful editorial guidance. Roma Gibson, at the BFI, found most of the illustrations and compiled the filmography at the back.

Finally, all of my friends who tolerated years of bad imitations and worse tap-dancing performances will be glad to know that I won't be watching any more musicals — at least not at the rate of ten per week.

For the second edition, I'd like to thank Alexander Doty, Edward Baron Turk and Janet Staiger for sharing their unpublished work on gay men as audiences for musicals with me, and the students in my 1989 Genre and Film seminar, in particular John Champagne, Matthew Tinkcom, Maureen Madison, Constance Mayer and Barbara White for contributions to my thinking about the new chapter.

The stage-within-a-
nightclub in **Go
Into Your Dance**

1:

Mass Art as Folk Art

The incredible thing about Jolson's career is that he
reached the highest rung of the show-business ladder without
benefit of the mass media that today can catapult a performer to
success.

Don Dunn, **The Making of No, No Nannette**
(Secaucus, NJ: Citadel Press, 1972) pp.138-9

It seems appropriate that both the Hollywood musical and
this book should begin with Al Jolson, for Jolson epitomized every
quality the Hollywood musical sought to appropriate from its live
ancestors. Charismatic entertainers — Jolson and Maurice Chevalier
were two of the earliest — tripped lightly from the music hall to the
movies, bringing with them a style of performing whose goal was
direct contact between performer and audience. In many of his films
Jolson played an entertainer based on his stage persona, the florid
style deriving its urgency from his effort to pierce through the barrier
of the screen. Within the films, the 'hard-sell' vaudeville personality,
the emotional excess (all derived from the blackface 'mammy-song'
tradition), contributed to an uninterrupted flow of energy from
performer to audience. As if still on the apron of the Winter Garden,
his 'home' on Broadway, Jolson in these early Hollywood musicals
created his act around audience-participation formats, singalongs or
requested numbers. The songs themselves were traditional tunes or
Jolson-identified standards — *Cielito Lindo* or a mammy song.

The very architecture of those arenas in which Jolson
performed thrust him into the heart of the audience. Just as on
Broadway, Jolson had built a special runway which jutted out into the
orchestra of the Winter Garden, so in his backstage films, Jolson
mingled with the night-club audience in a floor-show format. **Wonder
Bar** gave us Jolson as proprietor of a night club, reigning over his
entertainment kingdom, addressing specific lyrics to favored
customers. In **Go Into Your Dance**, Jolson conceived the 'Casino de
Paris,' a night club perched on tiers on a Broadway stage,
incorporating the informal night club atmosphere into a Broadway

1

show and the whole into a movie. In a similar way, Maurice Chevalier came to the movies (and to America) trademarks intact: the straw hat, the Gallic smirk, the sexual innuendo seemingly transferred whole to the screen. Chevalier was even permitted to break a Hollywood taboo by looking directly into the lens to address the cinema audience. In **One Hour With You,** Chevalier winked and leered into the lens as if letting the spectator in on a dirty joke.

It was the charisma of Jolson and Chevalier that these musical films of the early to mid-1930s attempted to transfer to the screen. Indeed the pioneering Vitaphone shorts of 1926-8 had been filmed records of musical performances — operatic, orchestral and vaudeville — just as the Lumière brothers had attempted to record the visible aura of ordinary life. One dominant impulse in musical films appears to be congenital: the desire to capture on celluloid the quality of live entertainment. Yet also from infancy, the dream of immediacy came up against the reality of technological truth: film is not a 'live' medium. Performances on film are recorded performances. Now the music-hall tradition itself had been founded upon an illusion that the audience really participated in the creation of Jolson's and Chevalier's highly calculated acts. In a sense the Hollywood musical merely compounded an already existing and widely accepted fiction, that of direct and spontaneous performance.

In a discussion of the evolution of British music hall, Stuart Hall and Paddy Whannel suggest that the emergence of stars marked the transition from 'folk' art to 'popular' art. The result of this shift, they claim, is that 'the community had become an "audience": the art had been individualized'. As Hall and Whannel describe it, popular art may have many things in common with folk art — in particular the direct contact between audience and performer — but it differs from folk art in that

the audience-as-community had come to depend on the performer's skills, and on the force of a personal style, to articulate its common values and interpret its experiences. ★

★ The Popular Arts (New York: Pantheon, 1965) pp.53-66

The Hollywood musical is one degree farther removed from 'folk' art in that it involves mechanical reproduction and mass distribution. From the movie musical's industrial origins stems an alienation between performer and audience that has both a sociological and an aesthetic dimension. The Hollywood musical shares with popular art a socio-economic alienation. Instead of a community where all, at least potentially, may perform, relations of production are alienated from those of consumption. The performers do not consume the product and the consumers do not produce it.

But with mechanical reproduction and mass distribution, 'alienation' takes on an aesthetic dimension as well. For with

★ See Walter
Benjamin, 'The
Work of Art in the
Age of Mechanical
Reproduction,' in
Illuminations
(New York:
Schocken, 1969).

reproduction the performer's presence, his 'aura', vanishes. ★ In the case of Al Jolson, the loss seems in retrospect an obvious and devastating one; he is simply too 'big' for the screen. Yet even for those performers seemingly made for the cinema — Astaire and Garland to name the most obvious — the loss of presence must be accounted as the perceptual and historical pre-condition for their screen images.

The Hollywood musical as a genre perceives the gap between producer and consumer, the breakdown of community designated by the very distinction between performer and audience, as a form of cinematic original sin. The musical seeks to bridge the gap by putting up 'community' as an ideal concept. In basing its value system on community, the producing and consuming functions severed by the passage of musical entertainment from folk to popular to mass status are rejoined through the genre's rhetoric. The musical, always reflecting back on itself, tries to compensate for its double whammy of alienation by creating humanistic 'folk' relations in the films; these folk relations in turn act to cancel out the economic values and relations associated with mass-produced art. Through such a rhetorical exchange, the creation of folk relations *in* the films cancels the mass entertainment substance *of* the films. The Hollywood musical becomes a mass art which aspires to the condition of a folk art, produced and consumed by the same integrated community. The remainder of this chapter takes up four aspects of folk-art creation for mass-art cancellation as reflected in the content of Hollywood musicals. These include the enshrining of spontaneous over engineered effects, the masking of choreography and rehearsals, the creation of amateur entertainment to cancel professionalism, and the creation of communities both offstage and backstage. Chapter 2 takes up the same issue of creation and cancellation in terms of cinematic form.

Bricolage vs Engineering

★ Michael Wood,
**America in
the Movies**
(New York:
Basic Books, 1975)
p.156

A whole batch of domestic objects is rounded up and danced with. These are precisely the connections that great musicals are always making; these are just the continuities they insist on; our speech can be nudged into music, our way of walking can be edged into a dance; and the things in our house are all possible props for an improvised ballet. ★

Michael Wood is describing Gene Kelly's and Donald O'Connor's spirited dance to *Moses Supposes* from **Singin' in the Rain**, yet he could just as easily be describing an entire category of

3

numbers in which performers make use of props at hand, things perhaps intended for other ends, to create the imaginary world of the musical number. Of course, the room furnishings and tools of the elocution teacher were not put there for Kelly's and O'Connor's choreographic pleasure. Yet they form the creative repository out of which the audience has come to expect a dance may be born. The very conventionality of the prop dance encourages us to suspend our disbelief regarding the reasons for the props being there. And if no props are at hand, the performer may simulate props using his body as a tool; whence the inclusion of mime in such numbers. Gene Kelly doesn't need props to become, say, an airplane or Charlie Chaplin (in **An American in Paris**).

'Tinkering' of this sort lends an irresistible aura of spontaneity to numbers which in reality are feats of technological know-how (as when Astaire dances on the walls and ceiling in **Royal Wedding**). The French anthropologist Claude Lévi-Strauss coined the term *bricolage* ('tinkering') to describe a similar makeshift tendency in the cognitive processes of pre-scientific cultures. In creating his cultural and intellectual artifacts primitive man makes use of materials at hand which may not bear any relationship to the intended project but which appear to be all he has to work with. Lévi-

Royal Wedding

★ C. Lévi-Strauss,
The Savage Mind,
translation ©
Weidenfeld &
Nicolson
(University of
Chicago Press, 1966)
p.17

Strauss contrasts the *bricoleur* of folk cultures to the goal-directed engineer of modern scientific thought whose tasks are subordinated to the availability of raw materials and tools conceived and procured for the purposes of the project. ★ In applying this distinction to **Singin' in the Rain**, one might say that Kelly's and O'Connor's number is carefully engineered to give an effect of *bricolage*. Engineering is a prerequisite for the creation of effects of utter spontaneity in the Hollywood musical. The *bricolage* number attempts to cancel engineering (a characteristic of mass production) by substituting *bricolage* (a characteristic of folk production).

For both Astaire and Kelly, props must not appear as props. Rather they must give the impression of being actual objects in the environment: a coat rack (Astaire in **Royal Wedding**) or a mop (Kelly in **Thousands Cheer**) will do as well as the girl herself. It was Astaire who pioneered and perfected the prop dance. Astaire dances with golf club and balls in **Carefree**, with firecrackers in **Holiday Inn**, and with a piano and some chairs in **Let's Dance**. In **Top Hat**, he uses his cane to gun down members of the audience. He dances on roller skates in **Shall We Dance** and on ice skates in **The Belle of New York**. In **Funny Face** he improvises a matador's sword and cape dance with his umbrella and raincoat. Astaire dances with photographs of the woman in **Broadway Melody of 1940, Royal Wedding,** and in the title number of **Funny Face**. Drums serve as dance props in *Nice Work if You Can Get It* (**A Damsel in Distress**); *Drum Crazy* (**Easter Parade**); and *History of the Beat* (**Daddy Longlegs**). In many of these numbers, Astaire creates the dance out of the total environment, giving an impression of spontaneous combustion. Dances of the 1930s sprung from the immediate environment include the boiler-room dance (*Slap That Bass*) in **Shall We Dance** and the funhouse sequence in **A Damsel in Distress**; the dance with the coat rack, metronome and exercise equipment in the ship's gym in **Royal Wedding** is a well-known example from Astaire's MGM period.

Gene Kelly has referred to an environmental conception for choreography as his 'hobby horse'. Kelly's development as a choreographer can be traced through his development of the *bricolage* number. In **Thousands Cheer**, Kelly uses a soda fountain and all its trimmings as the environment around which the choreography is created; this enables him to employ a mop (which just happens to be lying about) as his dancing partner. In **Living in a Big Way** Kelly creates dances around a statue and a dog, and around a building project, a natural environment from which children may be incorporated into the dance. Environment choreography abounds in the Kelly-Donen collaborations. *Prehistoric Man* (**On the Town**) makes a stage out of the Museum of Natural History. *Moses Supposes, Good*

5

Mornin', Make 'em Laugh, and the title number in **Singin' in the Rain** are all created around props at hand. When three men dance in the streets in **It's Always Fair Weather**, even garbage-can lids can become dance accessories. Of all Kelly's environmental conceptions, the one which gives the greatest impression of spontaneity springs from a stage's squeaky floor board and an old newspaper (**Summer Stock**). Here Kelly uses the proscenium stage not as an arena for the dance but rather as material for the dance. Astaire appeared to use the prop dance out of a kind of despair — no partner of flesh could match his grace. Kelly made of it a peculiarly American institution, giving *bricolage* the stamp of good old American inventiveness. But it is a number whose ostensible function is to satirize these MGM production numbers which, oddly enough, makes the most elaborate use of props at hand.

In **A Star is Born**, Judy Garland recreates at home a production number from a Hollywood musical in which her character in the film is starring. Garland uses only the props available in her living room to simulate the elaborate number: she turns on the lamp ('lights'), positions a table ('camera') and begins the 'action'. She uses the elastic bands of a chair for a harp, a pillow for an accordian, a lampshade for a coolie's hat, a leopard-skin rug for an African costume, the salt and pepper shakers for instruments in the Brazilian section. Her surprise at discovering each object at exactly the needed time makes us forget that these objects were carefully positioned there for her use. We get the impression that Judy Garland is rebuilding the phoney, calculated studio-production number around her own intimate environment. And yet this number is actually the most calculated of all. The more it appears as *bricolage,* the more it cancels out its creation through engineering.

Although they may appear polar opposites, the *bricolage* and the engineered number are actually closely related. Indeed many numbers (especially in MGM musicals) employ both. *Shoes with Wings On,* Astaire's animated number in **The Barkleys of Broadway**, needed elaborate process photography to create the effect of spontaneous dancing shoes, the objects in the immediate environment of the shoemaker Astaire portrays. In order for Astaire to dance on the walls and ceiling, trick photography must combine with tinkering as the woman's picture and a chair stand in for the object of affection. Even Kelly's apparently simple and spontaneous dance with the newspaper and the squeaky floor board could not have been achieved on a stage, precisely synchronized as it is to the music. Bricolage and engineering — at first glance, antitheses — become instead twin images of a paradox, for in the Hollywood studio film it takes engineering to give an effect of tinkering. And it takes a lot of

6

engineering to make the dance itself, rather than the gimmickry, noticeable to the audience. Engineering as the mode of production of the Hollywood musical is cancelled by a content relying heavily upon *bricolage*. We lose all sense of the calculation lying behind the numbers and we gain, as a bonus, the aura of absolute spontaneity. The number may appeal as 'folk' art while taking full advantage of the possibilities technology gives mass art.

Non-Choreography and Non-Rehearsals

Thus far I've discussed the overall conception of musical numbers as tinkering. But what of the content of the dancing itself? A brief excursion into dance history may be useful here. While it is quite true that all forms of dance employed in musicals have their origins in the 'folk', it is also true that the dominant dance styles in the 1930s' musicals — tap dancing ('hoofing') and ballroom dancing — reflected sub-cultures or European dance forms rather than the folk roots of the dominant American culture. The kind of dancing Astaire does is 'folk' in the sense of being more natural and spontaneous than classical ballet dancing (though in truth Astaire glosses vernacular dance styles with tinges of the classical vocabulary noticeable especially in his *port de bras,* his turns, his leaps and his partnering). But Astaire and Rogers do not appear 'folksy' to the audience; they are still too European for that. Curiously enough, it took a revolution in

7

ballet during the late 1930s and the war years to introduce American 'folk' ritual dancing into the Hollywood musical.

In the 1930s the musical either shunned ballet or made a travesty of it (as in the finale of **Shall We Dance** or Eleanor Powell's Pierrette dance on pointes in **Broadway Melody of 1940**). The handful of films George Balanchine choreographed were the exception, not the rule. Then ballet itself changed in such a way as to make itself accessible to Hollywood. Choreographers such as Eugene Loring (**Billy the Kid**), Agnes de Mille (**Rodeo**) and Jerome Robbins (**Fancy Free**) made what the dance critic Edwin Denby calls 'local colour' ballets out of American folk material — cowboys and sailors. Even more significantly these choreographers frequently dispensed with the unnatural classical line of ballet to introduce a more natural and spontaneous dance style based on American folk stance and gesture. The new choreographers had themselves been influenced by the labored but free movements of modern dance (notably the American themes of Martha Graham) and the psychological mime-ballets of Anthony Tudor. All of these influences combined to produce a new style of American ballet closer to acting than before, closer to natural body rhythms; as in the sequence in **Rodeo** when the boys dance out the riding of bucking broncos. With Agnes de Mille's dances for **Oklahoma!** on Broadway in 1943, the new choreography began to penetrate musical comedy, soon finding its way to the sound stages of MGM. Choreography for group dances in musicals of the 1940s borrows from the new ballet its incorporation of folk gesture flavored by frontier motifs. Choreography for the bricolage numbers borrows from the new ballet its conception of dancing as acting, the spontaneous outpouring of emotion. Even more than in the new ballet, dancing at MGM is rendered narrative and naturalized. If classical ballet seeks to conceal all effort, and modern dance seeks to reveal all effort, then musicals seem to want to naturalize all effort.

Agnes de Mille's dances for the 1955 film version of **Oklahoma!** epitomize the new 'folk' ballet

Clowning as dancing: *Too Bad We Can't Go Back to Moscow* from **Silk Stockings**

In prop numbers and elsewhere, Hollywood musicals employ choreography which could only by a great stretch of the imagination be called 'dancing'. Such 'non-choreography' implies that choreography is cancelled out — precisely the impression this dance style gives. By cancelling choreography as a calculated dance strategy, non-choreography implies that dancing is utterly natural and that dancing is easy. Both the group folk dance and the prop number reflect this view of the dance. The continuity between walking and dancing is always stressed. Dances which employ completely ordinary movements rather than 'steps' (for instance Bobby Van's jumping number from **Small Town Girl** featured in **That's Entertainment**) aim for an effect of natural body language within a loosely choreographed narrative framework. The frequent casting of non-dancers in Hollywood musicals leads to the creation of routines in which a thin line separates normal from choreographed movement. Clowning may compensate for the lack of choreography in the usual sense as in numbers featuring Jules Munshin in **On the Town** and *Too Bad We Can't Go Back to Moscow* in **Silk Stockings**. Or props may conceal the non-dancer, as in Kelly's getting-ready-to-leave-on-tour routine with Kay Kendall, some suitcases and a set of golf clubs in **Les Girls**.

Non-choreography reached its peak in MGM musicals of the 1950s. **It's Always Fair Weather** gives us Michael Kidd, Dan Dailey, and Gene Kelly, professional dancers all, romping about on the streets of New York. Unlike **On the Town**, where Kelly was teamed with Sinatra and Munshin, Kelly's and Donen's choreography didn't have to be adapted to non-dancers. Yet the dance appears resolutely amateurish, despite the technique involved. The men's movements

9

are ultra-spontaneous, bordering on ordinary horsing around. One segment consists of the everyday movement of running down the street; another segment seems to feature clumsiness as a prime choreographic element with the three buddies stomping 'gracelessly' about on garbage can lids. Each stamp of the men's feet cancels out that quality of grace associated with classical ballet and with the 1930s' figure of Astaire. By denying that numbers are choreographed, the Hollywood musical also denies work is involved in producing dance routines. MGM musicals aspire to the free and easy quality of folk dance.

This can be viewed with exceptional clarity in group dances explicitly given as community rituals (notably, the young people's segment from the *Fourth of July* sequence in the Mamoulian-directed **Summer Holiday** and the better-known *Skip to My Lou,* from **Meet Me in St Louis,** both mid-1940s MGM musicals choreographed by Charles Walters and inspired by de Mille's dances for **Oklahoma!**). *Skip to My Lou,* danced to the traditional folk song, achieves its fresh, unrehearsed quality by emerging imperceptibly from the natural groupings and movements at the party where it is danced. Boys and girls try out a few 'involuntary' steps which blend out of a moment of chaos into the dance proper. Narrative connections further naturalize the dance movements, as in the 'lost my partner' refrain, referring to Esther's interest in the boy next door. *Skip to My Lou* projects a folk quality through and through. Fiddle and ukelele lend a country flavor, bowed and strummed by the party-goers in that communal effort which defines folk art. All can participate in steps which are simple, natural and easily learned. The amateur group dance adds local color

to the palette of natural choreography in the Hollywood musical. The pure 'folk' performance represents the bottom line of audience manipulation in that performer and audience are one and the same. In the group folk dance, the choreographer is the community; in the MGM group folk dance the choreographer is Charles Walters masquerading as the community. MGM passes off the latter as the former; the choreography forces us to accept the illusion.

Non-choreography and folk choreography conceal the work of making dances. Another common deception of the Hollywood musical — the presentation of finished performances as rehearsals — conceals yet another truth about making entertainment. To quote Gene Kelly in **Summer Stock**, 'putting on a show is hard work'. In such bogus rehearsal scenes as the cat number in **Footlight Parade** (*Sitting on a Backyard Fence*) we get all the polish of a finished performance together with the casual quality of the rehearsal environment. The number commences with a shot of cast and crew observing the rehearsal, yet the number as we see it becomes a fully edited Busby Berkeley extravaganza identical to those presented in final shows.

Fred Astaire and Ginger Rogers would perform their most dazzling footwork under the guise of rehearsing. Rehearsal numbers — *I'll Be Hard to Handle* from **Roberta** and *I'm Putting All My Eggs in One Basket* from **Follow The Fleet** — come across as courtship rituals for the couple rather than performances for an audience. A danced dialogue appears to take place, and we forget that we are observing a carefully planned, executed and filmed performance. Even when the rehearsal atmosphere is stressed, as in the *Bouncin' the*

11

Blues practice session from **The Barkleys of Broadway,** the informal
elements (bare stage, Ginger's warm-up) are eclipsed by the exploding
(and perfectly coordinated) tap routine. Although spontaneity must
of necessity be ever an illusion in any film, the backstage musical
compounds the illusion by giving us 'improvisation' in a rehearsal
atmosphere.

     The same impulse appears to drive the masking of choreo-
graphy and the masking of rehearsals. Both serve to render *as*
entertainment the work that goes into producing entertainment. It is
not that choreography and rehearsals are eliminated from the endless

chronicle of putting on a show. There can be no cancellation without the initial creation. But the dances and the practicing of them are shown in such a way as to efface their own origins in labor (dancing and choreography) and in technology (filming). The process of creation and cancellation in turn renders transparent the creation of the Hollywood musicals themselves. An illusion of spontaneity ultimately serves to cancel out the place musicals occupy in the history of entertainment as mass art becomes folk art. We are never allowed to realize that musical entertainment is an industrial product and that putting on a show (or putting on a Hollywood musical) is a matter of a labor force producing a product for consumption. If we were to think about that, if we were to think at all, it wouldn't be entertainment any more. Nor do we contemplate the alienated quality of that consumption. We don't bow the fiddle; our pleasure is purchased from professionals. The whole notion of professional entertainment poses a problem for a mass art struggling to appear as a folk art.

Amateurs and Professionals

When Fred Astaire and Ginger Rogers do a number more dependent on virtuosity than romance, it's shown as part of an amateur ballroom-dancing competition (*Let Yourself Go* in **Follow the Fleet**). When Judy Garland stands up to sing in MGM musicals, more likely than not she's performing on an amateur basis at a party or in a barn rather than playing the Palace. When Gene Kelly is not dancing with Cyd Charisse or Leslie Caron, he is likely to be dancing with children (in **Living in a Big Way, Anchors Aweigh,** and **An American in Paris**). For a movie genre which itself represents professional entertainment and which is also frequently about professional entertainers, there seems to be a remarkable emphasis on the joys of being an amateur. To understand such an incongruity, it's instructive to recall the etymology of the word 'amateur' from the Latin, *amator,* lover. It is precisely the distinction between singing and dancing for the love of it, and singing and dancing for profit in a formal arena, that distinguishes the professional from the amateur entertainer. This means that all folk art is amateur entertainment. One of the reasons popular entertainment needs to redefine itself as folk art is to soften the harder edges of professionalism. Stardom came in with the emergence of popular and mass entertainment out of communal folk art. And the profit motive represents the economic side of such celebrity. Amateur entertainers, on the other hand, can't exploit us because they *are* us.

13

Wouldn't it be nice if we could combine the charisma of the professional with the folksiness of the amateur?

This is precisely what the Hollywood musical tries to do. By eliminating professionalism within the films, the more exploitative aspects of professionalism appear to be eliminated between the film and its spectator. Many musicals deal with the dilemma of professionalism by eliminating the backstage context entirely. In this way singing and dancing may emerge from the joys of ordinary life. In the 1940s there arose an entire sub-genre of Hollywood musicals taking place in small towns, the West or other 'folk' community settings. ★ In such locales — St Louis or even rural Brooklyn — amateur forms of entertainment often employing folk motifs could emerge naturally. More importantly the professional entertainer could play the part of the amateur without ever having to be truly amateurish. Indeed Gene Kelly built his career around such character roles.

★ My discussion of the folk musical is indebted to the unpublished and published work of Charles F. Altman. See *'Pour une étude sémantique / syntaxique du genre hollywoodien: le musical folklorique'*, **Ça/Cinéma**.

Perhaps the consummate example of the rhetorical gains such a situation may provide is the cakewalk number performed by Judy Garland and Margaret O'Brien in **Meet Me in St Louis**. No matter how many times one sees the film, this performance comes across as absolutely natural and spontaneous. Musicals go to great lengths to achieve an aura of amateurism. **Take Me Out to the Ball Game** finds an ingenious solution by taking as its heroes three professional ballplayers whose off-season love is vaudeville. Baseball is their job; vaudeville their recreation.

No performer in the Hollywood musical had more talent than Judy Garland, and no performer more frequently portrayed the amateur, a girl who sings for love instead of money. Judy Garland's

Meet Me in St Louis: *Under the Bamboo Tree*

child-like qualities were exploited in her films in order to lend an amateur feeling to all her performances. Even her vocal quality is kept within an amateur range; music critic Henry Pleasants has observed that Garland's singing voice had 'a sound innocent of anything that smacked of artful management'. ★ Even in backstage musicals, she was always the neophyte entertainer in the process of becoming professional, a star in the process of being born (archetypally in **Easter Parade** and **A Star is Born**). Garland portrays amateurs in her films with Mickey Rooney and in her folk musicals of the same period (**Little Nellie Kelly, Presenting Lily Mars**) and after (**The Harvey Girls, In the Good Old Summertime**). At one point in **The Harvey Girls** Garland even has a line to the effect that the amateur waitresses are 'no competition' for the professional saloon dance-hall girls across the way. But of course we know they are.

★ **The Great American Popular Singers** (New York: Simon & Schuster, 1974) p.286

Judy Garland and Gene Kelly were professionals because they had more star quality than we do; because they sang and danced better than us; and because they did it for our money. Having them portray amateurs cancels out their obvious professionalism and brings them closer to us. When Judy sings *Over the Rainbow,* when Gene sings and dances in the rain, we may even forget the price of admission. Who could begrudge the money paid for such privileged moments? And yet — despite the strongest impression to the contrary — we didn't create those moments, and in a sense we aren't participating in them either. Why, in musicals, do we so often feel that we *are* participating? It's true — as I'll show in the next chapter — that the musical developed a filmic vocabulary to create this almost kinetic sense of participation in the film audience. But it's also true that the creation of community within the films cancels out the loss of community between Hollywood and its audience.

The Folk Community and the Community Backstage

The title number in both stage and screen versions of **Oklahoma!** (1943 and 1955, respectively) celebrates simultaneously the union of Curly and Laurey and the incipient statehood of the Oklahoma territory. Paralleling the making of the couple with the making of a stable community is one sure sign of the folk sub-genre. We have already seen why folk musicals tend to use traditional group dances in lieu of more professional dance styles. The choreography blurs the dividing line between performer and audience, between principals and chorus in the dance, between audience and film, so that the dance may become a community ritual. The folk musical reeks with nostalgia for America's mythical communal past even as the musical itself exemplifies the new, alienated mass art.

Two song formats are used over and over again in these musicals to catch us up in the nostalgia. The singalong, a traditional form in ordinary life (hymn singing, campfire songs, following the bouncing ball), links entertainment to community. The audience really does produce the show in a singalong. The 'passed-along song', on the other hand, appears to be a specifically cinematic technique; we do not ordinarily see people passing songs along on the street (though the musical would have it so). **Meet Me in St Louis** commences with a passing along of the title song from family member to family member, snaking its way through the family manse. ★ **Love Me Tonight** treats the pass-along satirically as *Isn't It Romantic?* gets passed from Maurice Chevalier in his tailor's shop to Jeanette MacDonald in her chateau via such intermediaries as a band of gypsies and the entire French army. Passed-along numbers almost always employ film techniques such as the travelling shot and the montage sequence to illustrate the spread of music by the folk through the folk. Of the two techniques, the montage sequence has the greater capacity for demonstrating the diffusion of entertainment on a considerably grander scale than the Smith family.

In **The Story of Vernon and Irene Castle**, an unusually long and elaborate montage sequence detailing the couple's rise to fame climaxes with a shot of Fred and Ginger (as Vernon and Irene) dancing over a gigantic map of the United States. As the couple dances from city to city, miniature circles of tiny dancing couples spring up at each

★ Other examples of passed-along songs include: *On the Acheson, Topeka and the Santa Fe* (**The Harvey Girls**); *It's a Lovely Day for a Wedding* (**Royal Wedding**); *This is a Day for Love* (**Yolanda and the Thief**). Passed-along songs original to the films in which they are sung but imitative in form or function of *Meet Me in St Louis* include *I Was Up with the Lark This Morning* in **Centennial Summer** (1946), a waltz; *Our State Fair* in **State Fair** (1945), a fair song; and *Our Home Town* in **Summer Holiday** (1946), a home-town place-name song.

The Story of Vernon and Irene Castle

city, dancing to a song associated with that locale (*Hello Frisco, Hello, Chicago, Way Down Yonder in New Orleans*). By the end of the sequence the entire United States map is covered with singing and dancing couples. **Lady Be Good** uses a common variant of the rise-to-fame montage: the rise to the top of the charts of the title song. We are shown how the familiar Gershwin tune (presumably just composed by the husband and wife song-writing team in the film) spreads through various ethnic groups, languages and nationalities. Not only is *Lady Be Good* a contagious 'folk' phenomenon, it is international in scope, making of the entire world a community through song. The fact that **Lady Be Good** is also the title of the film helps make the analogy between the montage sequence within the film and the hoped-for effects of the film itself. Entertainment products are communally produced and consumed yet diffused through mass media. Mass distribution becomes a blessing rather than a curse.

In backstage musicals the spectacle of a global community of singing and dancing folk gets mirrored within the films proper. The world of the stage is a community too, the films seem to say. The cooperative effort that goes into putting on a show is extended to include the film's audience. Folk numbers and folk motifs find their way into the shows themselves as if in celebration of the community backstage. The cinema audience feels a tremendous sense of participation in the team effort, cancelling out the alienation inherent in the viewing situation.

Warner Bros musicals of the early 1930s place a premium on cooperation and group participation in the success of the final show. The anonymous spectacle of the Busby Berkeley production number would seem to celebrate collective endeavor. Often the plots of these backstage vehicles take as their theme the need for community within the world of the stage. Within the society of the theatrical company, personal greed (usually embodied in a temperamental star) may stand as an obstacle to the show's success; meanwhile, outside forces may be working to undermine the collective endeavor that is the show. In **Footlight Parade**, a company member leaks Cagney's ideas to a rival producer; in **Dames**, a prudish and hypocritical moral society wants to censor the show; in **Gold Diggers of 1933** the Depression itself cripples the production. But in the always ultimately successful effort to put on the show, the theatrical community overcomes all foes. Over and over again in these backstage films we see the 'kids' triumphing over greed, egotism and all those puritanical forces which would, in the name of the community, conspire against entertainment. The Mickey Rooney - Judy Garland vehicles seem to be cut from the same cloth.

But the film which deals most explicitly with these themes must surely be **The Band Wagon,** an apology for the classic backstage musical coming near the end of its long run (1953). The film gives us two shows, each called 'The Band Wagon'; the first 'Band Wagon' seems to exist solely in order that we may contrast it with the second, successful version. We never see a completed number from the first 'Band Wagon', a musical version of Faust with 'meaning and stature'. Even the dress rehearsal quite literally goes up in smoke; the show itself is symbolized by the enormous egg we are led to believe it lays. Lorded over by the pretentious actor-writer-director Jeffrey Cordova, the first production serves as Exhibit A for the wrong way to put on a show. Cordova fails, we are led to believe, because he is insensitive to the company and to the audience. By contrast, stardom does not distance Tony Hunter (Astaire) who masterminds the second (though in fact it's the original musical comedy) version of 'The Band Wagon', the one we actually get to see at the end. Although Tony starts out 'by himself, alone', he soon realizes the only way to make a comeback is by renewing his relationship with a live audience; this Tony accomplishes by dancing with a shoe-shine man at the scene of his latter-day theatrical triumphs, now transformed into a garish arcade. Yet at the end of the dance, when the mysterious machine bursts open and his audience rushes to congratulate him, we feel that Tony/Astaire has indeed come back to us. The first production, riddled as it is with interpersonal conflicts and hilarious technical difficulties, seems in retrospect but a detour in Tony's awareness. Conflict with his leading lady Gabrielle (Cyd Charrise), a smug ballerina in her first Broadway show, is resolved by dancing in the dark, just as they've observed the simple folk doing. After finding himself the only guest at the official cast party, Tony adjourns to the real cast party, the chorus party, where the company improvises a performance of *I Love Louisa*, presumably a number from one of Tony's old and great audience favorites (in fact Astaire did it in the 1929 Broadway revue **The Band Wagon**). Prior to this turning point, we've observed the ballerina isolating herself from the group, an artist among hoofers. Now she blends with the chorus, dancing their steps with one of the boys as partner. Not even the camera singles her out. Several numbers in the final, smash-hit show seem almost a tribute to the theatrical community. The opening *New Sun in the Sky* seems to symbolize Gaby's rebirth. *Louisiana Hayride,* a country-folksy production number, has Nanette Fabray calling out the roll of the chorus, as if acknowledging the 'folk' of the theatrical community.

 Hayride provides a good example of a trend in backstage musicals of the 1940s and 1950s related to the emergence of the folk musical proper: the creation of numbers with 'folk' motifs in the final shows of backstage musicals. *Hoe Down* from **Babes on Broadway** is an early instance of a square-dance pattern in a show within a totally

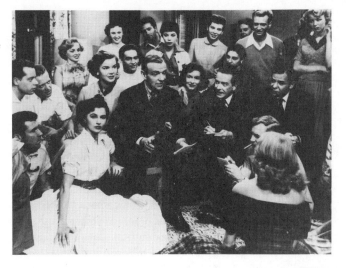

urban backstage plot; *Louisiana Hayride* takes the country motif into
the 1950s. Even Astaire gets into the act: dressed up as a tramp in *A
Couple of Swells*; as a low-life in **Royal Wedding**. Judy Garland plays
a farmer in **Summer Stock**; and in her opening number in **Easter
Parade** wishes she were back in Michigan, 'down on the farm'.

All these onstage numbers with folk themes should call to
mind an archetypal backstage musical plot so common it seems in
retrospect to be parodying itself: the one where the small-town girl
comes to New York to try for that big break in a Broadway show. The
girl in the backstage musical need not come from Iowa (as she does in

19

the stage spoof of such stories, **Dames at Sea**), but she must have her roots in the provinces. If in **Broadway Melody of 1936**, Eleanor Powell comes from Albany, then Albany must come to represent the small town back home. **On the Town** seems to expand its entire rhetoric upon transforming New York City into Meadowville, Indiana, a friendly, folksy place. And it must be remembered that 'it happened in Brooklyn', not Manhattan. The relevance of this pervasive plot to the theme of community in the backstage musical is evident: even after the girl becomes a star on Broadway (a professional entertainer), she retains an identity with rural America which rubs off on the alienated world of show business. **Easter Parade** insists on such a trade-off, as does **Summer Stock**, a fascinating and undervalued 1950 MGM musical. **Summer Stock** is unique among musicals of its period in achieving a fifty/fifty blend of folk and backstage themes. The film's plot redefines professional entertainment as putting on a show in a barn; its final production provides a textbook for the incorporation of folk motifs into the show.

This particular show, 'Fall in Love', opens with Judy Garland and Gene Kelly backed by the chorus. They hold out to their audience the ultimate promise musical comedy makes — that the dream of the show we're about to see and the dream of romance in that show are, as the song says, all for us. The opener has Kelly in Astaire's clothing, the top hat, white tie and tails of the professional dancer. But the song itself is passed among the cast. And the show's second number features the couple in candy-striped turn-of-the-century garb seemingly left over from the wardrobe for **Meet Me in St Louis**. The song they sing in these garments, *You Wonderful You*, would be a throw-away were it not a reprise of a plot-song earlier in the film. In its first rendition, *You Wonderful You* introduced the bucolic Garland to the joys of professional entertainment. Through the agency of the song, Kelly taught Garland that ultimate truth about musical comedy: even professionals are in it for love. Kelly reprised the song all by himself, whistling the fluffy little tune while dancing with the newspaper and squeaky floor board. In this wonderfully spontaneous moment, all the work of putting on the show seemed to evaporate. Now, in its second reprise in the final show, all its former meanings accrue to this airiest of melodies: love of performing, love of the audience, love between Kelly and Garland and, as a bonus, the reprise profits from that aura of community that the barn environment always lends to a performance.

After one of those folksy interludes — a hillbilly number reminiscent in style if not in quality of *A Couple of Swells* — we get the ultimate in professional entertainment, Garland's well-known *Get Happy*. In keeping with the folk / professional alternation observed

Folk motifs in the
final show of
Summer Stock

thus far, the finale is folk all the way home. Once again the song is a reprise of a plot-song, and once again it's given the full 'folk' rendition with full cast and chorus. In its previous version, the number (*Howdy Neighbor, Happy Harvest*) celebrated Garland's communal country roots as she sang to her neighbors of her acquisition of a tractor. But at that point in the film, the spirit of community was hostile to the spirit of entertainment. Now, in the final show, a curious blend is being celebrated; the folk elements are getting grafted upon the professional Broadway show, just as farmer Garland and performer Kelly are being united in love. The finale, so typical of musicals of this period, drives home the synthesis involved. Kelly and Garland stand before the chorus, arms raised to the audience (or is it to the heavens?) for the final refrain:

> *Remember neighbors when you work for Mother Nature*
> *You get paid by Father Time.*

A cut to a closer shot has eliminated from the frame the audience in the barn, so that these last lines of the finale are addressed directly to the cinema audience, almost palpably located in the offscreen space to the front of the stage. We are being invited to participate in a harvest ritual, a condensed version of **Oklahoma!** as it were, taking place as the finale of a Broadway show. Any distance

21

between us and them has been eliminated. At the same time and via the same rhetoric, the economic agreement between spectator and entertainment institution (i.e. Hollywood) is being renegotiated. Instead of working for MGM and getting paid by the spectators, the song claims that performer and audience alike are working for Mother Nature and getting paid by Father Time. Economic relations underlying professional entertainment and mass art are universalized, given the timeless and spiritual dimension of pre-industrial communities and of the folk arts. The final song of **Summer Stock** says this loud and clear. But it's cinematic technique that makes sure we'll listen to the words of the song without ever really hearing them. Conventions for staging and filming numbers in musicals position the spectator as an uncritical consumer of entertainment as folk rather than mass art.

Spectators and Spectacles

The personality of the dancer is missing in pictures.
You're with the audience in the theater. You look at them and you
can embrace them and they can embrace you, so to speak, or you
can hate each other. But you get no direct response from the screen.
It is so remote from the empathy of live theatre.

Gene Kelly, quoted in Donald Knox, **The Magic Factory**
(New York: Praeger. 1973) p.47

The Proscenium and the World Outside

The Hollywood musical worships live entertainment because live
forms seem to speak more directly to the spectator. To make a verbal
analogy, live entertainment seems to be a 'first-person' form, a
performance which assumes an active and present spectator. The
typical story film, on the other hand, is more like a third-person
narration the audience eavesdrops on. It is not a direct dialogue
between performer and audience. Maybe that's why so many musicals
are about putting on a show rather than about making films. Popular
theater has an immediacy and flexibility that the film medium lacks.
You can take a show on the road, try it out on real live audiences; if
necessary, as in **The Band Wagon,** you can throw out a bad show and
replace it with one the audience likes.

At this point, however, we are met with a contradiction. It is
true that in putting on a show the proscenium stage within the
backstage musical may provide an arena for dialogue. Yet as we have
already observed, the proscenium arch may also be perceived as a
barrier to direct communication. Hence the many attempts to
overcome this barrier: by turning the stage into a nightclub, by
dispensing with the stage altogether, by putting on shows in barns, and
so forth. And yet in those musicals in which 'the world is a stage', in
which performances are part of the narrative, proscenium or stage-
like arenas are often *created*. In **Meet Me in St Louis,** for example,
every musical performance is either framed or placed on a stage-like
platform. In *The Boy Next Door* and *Have Yourself a Merry Little
Christmas,* Judy Garland is framed by windows. In the cakewalk

23

number, she and Margaret O'Brien consciously use the arch created
by the passage into the dining area as a proscenium arch. In *The
Trolley Song* the moving trolley serves as platform. Far from wanting
to eliminate stages entirely, **Meet Me in St Louis** seems to want to put
stages where there are none. And in truth, whenever a number
commences in any musical, the world does become a stage. The
proscenium seems to occupy an ambiguous position in the musical
film. In musicals in which the stage is a world (backstage musicals), the
proscenium is perceived as a barrier and every attempt is made to
bridge the distance it creates. But when performance is taken outside
the theater, the proscenium is reborn out of ordinary space and the
world is a stage.

Such a duality is part of the history of the genre, since
musicals with performances integrated into the narrative developed
alongside those with proscenium performances. Indeed many films
include both types. The three major musical-producing studios of the
1930s (Warner Bros, MGM and RKO) almost always included narrative numbers in those films which featured professional entertainers,
and more formal performances in those films in which the leads were
non-entertainers or amateurs. Warners' backstage musicals had
courtship numbers taking place outside the theater (for example
Going Shopping with You in **Gold Diggers of 1935**). And MGM's
MacDonald-Eddy operettas, spin-offs from the earlier Paramount
operettas with MacDonald and Chevalier, almost always showed at
least one of the duo performing for an audience in the film.
MacDonald's opening aria in **New Moon** is performed for the elegant
society of first-class passengers aboard a ship. When Jeanette

MacDonald at long last discovers the proper lyrics for *Ah Sweet Mystery of Life* in **Naughty Marietta**, she trills them at another formal though amateur gathering.

It was the third of the major musical cycles of the 1930s, the Astaire-Rogers series at RKO, however, that contained the most complex interplay between proscenium numbers and narrative numbers. Indeed, in this series the original distinction between onstage and offstage itself begins to break down. **Top Hat** — to pick an example familiar to most — alternately creates and reduces proscenium distance. *No Strings,* the first musical number, is clearly narrative, introducing the Astaire figure and initiating the conflict with Rogers. The second number, the duet *Isn't This a Lovely Day (To Be Caught in the Rain),* brings the couple together within a stage-like space created by the bandstand under which they take shelter and upon which they dance. Astaire's *Top Hat, White Tie and Tails* is part of a musical show, yet there's some direct address to the audience; at one point Astaire 'shoots' the internal audience with his cane. *Cheek to Cheek* and *The Piccolino*, the last two numbers in **Top Hat,** take place at the night club in Venice. As for Jolson, the night club has a more open design than does the proscenium arch and tends to create less audience distance. It's an intermediate structure, somewhere between a stage and a world. And in *Cheek to Cheek* the night-club floor becomes a world as Astaire and Rogers whirl off into a secluded space. **Top Hat,** like so many other musicals, blends worlds and stages, reduces stages and makes stages of worlds. One might say that in **Top Hat** stages are created in order to be cancelled; distance is set up

The world as stage
in **Top Hat**

25

so that the film may bridge it. One needs a gap to close one. In *Top Hat, White Tie, and Tails,* the stage is quite visibly present but the staging of the number and the direct address to the audience render it impotent to create a barrier. *Isn't It a Lovely Day* needs to create a stage for Astaire and Rogers to make a world of by falling in love. Stages appear and disappear, proving again and again that the stage is a world we needn't feel any distance from and that the world is full of the spirit of musical comedy. The performers are part of our world and we're right up there on the screen.

The Audience in the Film

The Theatrical Audience ★

★ I shall use the terms 'internal audience' and 'theatrical audience' to refer to the audience *in* the films; the terms 'spectator' and 'film audience' to refer to the audience *of* the films.

Dwight MacDonald, in his infamous attack on popular culture, bemoans the fact that 'kitsch', as he puts it, 'includes the spectator's reactions in the work of art itself instead of forcing him to make his own responses'. ★ ★ One assumes MacDonald meant this metaphorically, but it would seem that the Hollywood musical takes him quite literally. Long before television invented the studio audience and canned laughter, the Hollywood musical was putting audiences into the film for the purpose of shaping the responses of the movie audience to the film. After 1933 it is unusual to find an onstage performance in a musical that does not include shots of applauding audiences in the theater. One could say that the internal audience in musicals, like the studio audience and canned laughter on television, are latter-day versions of the old theatrical claque. But this begs the question of the essential difference between 'stooges' in a theater and the new media derivatives of the stooge: one is live and the other isn't. Seeing the internal audience as compensation for a lost liveness puts it in a new and more meaningful perspective. In order to get a direct response from the film audience, Hollywood musical-makers had to place in their path another, spectral audience. Although even today movie audiences will frequently applaud numbers in musicals, there is always an uncanny ring to it, as anyone who has witnessed this phenomenon can testify. It's just unnatural to applaud those unhearing celluloid ghosts, even though your fellow audience members can hear you. But the audience in the film makes of the movie audience a live audience.

★ ★ 'A Theory of Mass Culture', **Diogenes,** No.3 (Summer 1953); reprinted in Bernard Rosenberg and David Manning White (eds), **Mass Culture: The Popular Arts in America** (New York: Free Press, 1957) p.61

    The final show of **Summer Stock** uses the audience in the barn in this fashion. We see the folk audience responding emphatically to professional entertainment; then through the cut in to a

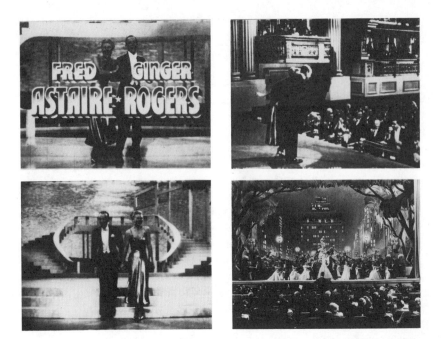

The Barkleys of Broadway

closer view of the stage, we take the place of that folk audience. In this way our subjectivity is placed within the narrative universe of the film. Film editing has the power to help us arrive at responses the internal audience presumably came to spontaneously. In the opening sequence of **The Barkleys of Broadway,** for instance, Fred Astaire and Ginger Rogers dance *Swing Trot,* a routine designed to arouse nostalgia for the famous team, together again for the first time in ten years. The couple is preserved in a golden picture-frame proscenium as they dance one of their old routines to a choir admonishing us to 'remember **Swing Time**'. At the end of the number, a cut to a shot from the point of view of the theater's wings reveals the couple taking a bow before a live audience. And in the next shot, we see Astaire's and Rogers' curtain speech from the point of view of that live audience. The audience in the film seems to be there to express the nostalgia the number itself sought to arouse in us. For how could the theatrical audience have known that Josh and Dinah Barkley are really good old Fred and Ginger? Clearly the internal audience serves a symbolic not a realistic purpose; they are the celluloid embodiment of the film audience's subjectivity.

After watching a hundred or so of these backstage musicals, one begins to see a pattern that operates above and beyond individual variations. Through shot transitions (rather than through any particular shot) the spectator may be included in the internal audience;

or he/she may replace the internal audience or both. In each case it's the intrusion of the internal audience between us and the performance which, paradoxically, gives the effect of a lived — and more significantly — a *shared* experience (for, of course, the experience of the film is lived in its own way). The conventional camera location for recording an onstage performance in a backstage musical was from an imaginary third-row-center seat within the audience. The resulting shot over the backs of the first few rows of the audience onto the stage (especially when projected upon the enormous screens of the past) gave the spectator the illusion of sitting adjacent to the internal audience, perhaps in the fourth row. We sense the spatial continuity from theater seats to movie-theater seats. Such an effect can be especially startling in musicals involving a film-within-a-film (say, the premières in **Singin' in the Rain** or **A Star is Born**, 1954) where the impression of participation this shot gives is even greater.

The shot which includes the spectator in the theatrical audience is never used alone, however, because once our subjectivity is established within the internal audience, we need to see more closely what that audience is seeing. Typically, there will be a cut to a closer view of the performance taken from the theater audience's point of view but eliminating them from the frame. In this second shot (or more properly in the effect of the cut to this shot) the spectator replaces the internal audience. The subjectivity of the spectator stands in for that of the spectral audience, rendering the performance utterly theatrical. We are, as it were, lifted out of the audience we actually belong to (the cinema audience) and transported into another audience, one at once more alive and more ghostly. And, in the cut to a closer shot, since the internal audience retreats into offscreen space, the performance can be truly 'all for us'.

This is the basic pattern, one so seemingly simple and conventional that we never stop to contemplate the perceptually quite complex sleight of hand involved. Of course there are variations on this pattern. Many musicals will dolly in and out from one shot to the next, preferring the less abrupt transition and increased subjectivity the moving camera gives. Director Vincente Minnelli liked to crane in over the backs of the audience at the start of a number so that when he craned up and all the way in at the climax, the camera movement would seem to be motivated by our subjective desires. The 1936 **Show Boat** uses long sweeping pans and even shots from over the backs of the audience in the balcony and the audience in the box seats. Whatever the technique, the effect is the same: to constantly remind the spectator that he/she is seeing from the point of view of the theatrical audience while at the same time moving in to address the performance directly to the spectator. Through a dialectic of presence and absence, inclusion and replacement, we may come to feel that we are at a live performance.

During the numbers, then, we are encouraged to identify with the audience in the film, to regain that precious live aura. Yet the backstage musical is more than just onstage performances. Only the numbers attempt to achieve an illusion of live entertainment; the plots follow the pattern of traditional Hollywood narrative in which we, the film audience, look onto the story from a position outside it. The story is told to us by the camera in a more impersonal 'third-person' mode. During the stories, however, we are encouraged to identify with the performer protagonists who, after all, are the heroes of these backstage sagas. To this end, subjective camera techniques may be used (the shot-reverse shot pattern is a staple of classical narrative) but always so that we may share the point of view of the performers. During the narrative interludes, then, we are encouraged to share the point of view of the performers, but during the musical interludes, we are encouraged to actually become part of the audience in the film — a very different and much closer type of identification.

But this is not the whole story. For, since the perspective of the performers has already been established through the narrative (or through our prior acquaintance with the film's stars), it is perfectly possible for us to experience a doubled or split identification during the performance without ever experiencing this split in our consciousness as disconcerting. When, usually during the curtain calls, we see the internal audience from the point of view of the performers, we do not lose our sense of identification with the live audience. In **Show Boat** we frequently peer out over the footlights into the mirror of our 'folk' counterparts. Indeed a shot-reverse shot pattern, which alternates the point of view of the internal audience with that of the performers, is a common means of getting us back and forth from the performance to the narrative. Nor does another typical angle — from the wings of the theater onto the stage — disorient us, for we already identify with one of the performers standing in the wings, whose view we are asked to share. The opening sequence of **A Star is Born** provides a virtual glossary of all these different points of view, and we have no trouble following it. Nor does it appear odd when, in **Broadway Melody of 1940**, we watch Eleanor Powell's performance from the point of view of Astaire standing at the back of the orchestra seats; or when, in **The Band Wagon**, we get a similar Astaire perspective on ballerina Cyd Charisse.

Yet in a literal sense, these rapid shifts of viewpoints do splinter our identification during a proscenium performance. Our view of the show is like that of a Cubist painting compared to the fixed positioning and fixed identification of the audience in the film. It is the

The wings shot in **A Star is Born**

narrative that holds it all together for us. Far from being the removable connective tissue many critics imply it is, the story of a backstage musical is essential to our mode of experiencing the seeming heart of the musical — the numbers. One has only to experience an early musical with a revue format or MGM's **Ziegfeld Follies** or the compilation film **That's Entertainment** to realize how much has been lost when the backstage context is excised.

The doubled identification provided by the musical's dual registers gives a tremendous rhetorical advantage. We feel a sense of participation in the creation of entertainment (from sharing the perspective of the performers) and, at the same time, we feel part of the live audience in the theater. Only a reflexive form such as the musical can lend so much intensity to our experience of a simple song and dance. The greatest musicals knew how to transform the entire tone of a number by playing one register against the other. **An American in Paris** features Gene Kelly and Georges Guetary in a typical, happy-to-be-in-love song and dance to Gershwin's *S'Wonderful*. At the end of the number the camera cranes majestically upward as what appears to be the entire population of Paris cheers the light-hearted performance. Only we, the audience of the film, know that the two men are singing about the same girl. Even a mediocre film can profit from the doubled identification, as when Judy Garland, swollen with unrequited love for Gene Kelly, goes out on stage to sing a poignant *After You've Gone* in **For Me and My Gal**. The cinema takes away aura, but she also gives it back. As a reflexive form, the musical can compensate for the distance it inevitably imposes as mass art. There may be a difference between a live performance and the illusion of one, but in the Hollywood musical, we're not allowed to notice it.

The Narrative Audience

Despite the most valiant attempts to bring us closer to the stage, the proscenium limits our sense of participation in the performance itself. A skillful director may use the camera to animate such performances, but (with the exception of Busby Berkeley for whom the proscenium was a joke) we remain aware that the performers are up there on the stage and we are down here in the audience. We may hope that Gene or Judy will succeed; we rarely hope that 'we' will succeed. But when the performance is a spontaneous one taking place in the realm of the narrative, we may experience a strong desire to sing and dance in the rain ourselves. Spurred on by the directorial brilliance of Vincente Minnelli and the persona of Gene Kelly, MGM musicals of the 1940s began to create natural audiences that would spontaneously gather around the impromptu numbers of an Astaire or a Kelly. The entire population of a Caribbean port city gathers to watch Gene Kelly search for his 'Nina' in **The Pirate**. In **An American in Paris** the folk of Paris seem to linger in the streets in the hope that Gene Kelly will perform for them: *By Strauss, I Got Rhythm,* and *S'Wonderful* are their reward. Gene Kelly likes himself as he roller skates through midtown Manhattan in **It's Always Fair Weather**; the somewhat aghast crowd that gathers to gape at him appears to like him too. When Gene Kelly dances with an old lady in *By Strauss,* or when Fred Astaire dances with the shoe-shine man in *Shine on Your Shoes,* not only does the audience appear to form spontaneously but also we are given an ordinary spectator-in-the-film, a non-dancer like us but one who's right up there performing nonetheless.

'Natural' audiences in **An American in Paris**

A closer look at one of these numbers — *By Strauss* — may reveal some of the secrets buried within those spontaneously generated crowds. *By Strauss* mocks Viennese waltzes through the clowning antics of the three major participants (Gene Kelly, Oscar Levant, Georges Guetary). The Parisian café setting provides the perfect forum for audience participation. For the first rendition of the song by the three men, Minnelli uses two basic camera set-ups, each the reverse shot of the other. In the first shot we look onto Oscar Levant at the piano in the lower right portion of the frame with Guetary and Kelly to his left. In the reverse shot we are able to see past Levant at the piano and through an open-arch doorway onto the busy Paris street. Minnelli stages and shoots in such a way that the arch assumes the guise of a natural proscenium, open in both directions. The first shot comes to represent the point of view of the street audience looking onto the performance, a point of view the spectator easily assumes. The second shot, over the performers and out through the arch, reminds us that performers and audience occupy the same space with no scenic barriers placed between them.

During a second chorus of the song, an audience consisting of the male and female proprietors of the café and the elderly proprietress of a flower shop wander in and are incorporated into the number. Until this point Minnelli has maintained a separation

32

An American in
Paris

between performers and audience through his shot-reverse shot set-ups. Some interplay occurs when the three new observers participate in the clowning. Now significant camera movement begins to blur the division between performers and audience. As Gene Kelly rises to waltz with the elderly woman, we are able to view the street audience to the right of the frame through the open arch. Later, as the camera cranes out through the arch, the interior 'audience' remains to the rear of Kelly and his partner but the outside audience is now framed to the right of the dancing couple. The camera movement has unobtrusively created a situation whereby the couple is flanked by an 'audience' on

both sides, and some members of that audience also qualify as performers. As the camera swings laterally back and forth to capture the graceful pas de deux it gives us a peek at the audience surrounding the dancing couple. Inside and outside space have merged into a community celebration.

Kelly then dances with both women, his audience singing along. All take part in the finale, ending with a shout of 'By Strauss' and applause. The number fades out on the principals posing for the street audience, but the applause comes from the direction of the offscreen space the street audience now occupies. We, the spectators, are encouraged to identify with a spontaneous audience which has actually participated in the performance.

It has been said that Minnelli made the camera dance along with the performers. But that is not the only lesson directors of musicals in the 1940s and 1950s learned from Minnelli. For, when Minnelli's camera danced, it most often danced in the service of subjectivity. The camera moves to bring us closer to the dance, but also to bring us to a subjective viewpoint from within the narrative's space. The same may be said for the cuts and camera set-ups in a number such as *By Strauss*. Minnelli rarely filmed a number in one take as was common at RKO in the 1930s; he knew this would limit the means not of showing us the dance but rather of involving us in it.

Direct Address:
Celebrating Entertainment

Every time there is a cut to a view of the performance alone in a backstage musical, we feel that the performance is being addressed directly to us. No matter how involved we become in the narrative of a musical, we do not get the same feeling of a scene being spoken for us and to us. Since the musical borrows its proscenium performances from live entertainment, the shift to direct address does not strike us as odd; it seems very natural. Yet direct address is often cited as one of the chief means of 'distanciation' in modernist theater and film.

I have been using the concept of 'distance' in the sense of 'aesthetic distance', the idea that the art object is a self-contained whole quite apart from its relationship to the beholder. It's the attitude we're supposed to bring to great paintings; we contemplate them in awe, but they're not supposed to talk back to us. Popular entertainment has goals diametrically opposed to the notion of art as object. Al Jolson does not present himself to us as an object for contemplation. His art is the art of dialogue, not monologue. Musical entertainment concentrates on breaking down any perceived distance between performer and audience.

When direct address is described as 'distanciation', however, something a little different is meant. This other sense of distancing is derived from the theater of Bertolt Brecht and has taken on prominence in film criticism in descriptions of, especially, the films of Jean-Luc Godard. 'Distanciation', 'estrangement', and 'alienation effect' refer to techniques whereby the spectator is lifted out of her transparent identification with the story and forced to concentrate instead on the artifice through which the play or film has been made. To this end Godard will call attention to the very things Hollywood movies seek to cover up. His actors will refer to the fact that they are in a movie; the soundtrack will blare up at inopportune moments; cuts which are 'invisible' in Hollywood movies will jar rather than flow together into a seamless rendering of the story; indeed the story itself will be no more than a series of digressions and allusions.

When Godard uses direct address, as he frequently does, he means it to be a direct statement to the spectator. A character may break out of the narrative to say a few words to us; or some third-world representatives may give long revolutionary speeches in the middle of a story about a husband and wife going away for the weekend. In order for Godard's distancing techniques to work, he has to assume that everyone is acquainted with the rules of classical Hollywood film-making. One of those rules is that the story should unfold in the 'third person' as it were, addressed to us but in such a way that we are

Direct address in
Tout Va Bien

enveloped in the narrative universe of the film. When a character in Godard addresses us directly, he breaks the narrative surface, and this makes us aware that we are watching a created fiction, not a world of dreams whole in itself. The Platonic ideal of a Hollywood film is one in which the audience perceives even the celluloid stock as the stuff of magic and the story as transcending its origin in light and shadow. The narratives of musical films exemplify this classical pattern. But the musical numbers regularly and systematically violate the smooth surface. The goals of musicals and those of Godard must surely be opposed. But — as in the case of direct address — their methods are identical. How can this be?

I believe the difference lies in what is being conveyed by the direct address and the traditions behind those messages. The narratives of musicals place themselves firmly within a long tradition of popular entertainment; we have seen that the musical views itself in direct line of descent from folk art. Godard, on the other hand, places himself in a dialectical relationship to Hollywood; he is the antithesis to which the narratives of musicals are the thesis. When performers in musicals turn to face us directly, we do enter another register, but as we have seen, the potentially disorienting effects of the break in narrative are minimized — by the presence of the audience in the film and by mechanisms of identification. Even when the break in register does throw us out of the narrative it's for the purpose of praising show business, not burying it.

One category of number that I'll call the 'Ode to Entertainment' almost always makes us pause to consider what the musical is all about. ★ Always built around a song lyric telling us

★ Material on the reflexive song lyric is in Chapter 3. Examples of 'Ode to Entertainment' numbers from MGM musicals include *Be a Clown* in **The Pirate**; the finale to **Take Me Out to the Ball Game**; *There's No Business Like Show Business* in **Annie Get Your Gun**; *You Wonderful You* in **Summer Stock**; *Make 'Em Laugh* in **Singin' in the Rain**; *Applause, Applause* in **Give a Girl a Break**; *That's Entertainment* in **The Band Wagon**; and *Stereophonic Sound* in **Silk Stockings**. Examples from other studios include *Dames* from **Dames** (Warners) and *There's No Business Like Show Business* from the Fox film of the same title.

there's no business like show business, the message is given in direct address. The ode to entertainment almost always occupies the finale position, coming at the summit of the show, the culmination of all the narrative energy the film posseses. The finale may be a reprise of the same song presented in a less direct manner earlier in the show — *Be a Clown* in **The Pirate** or *That's Entertainment* in **The Band Wagon**. Wherever such numbers occur, they always serve a finale function, including us in the celebration of another entertainment triumph. We're always at a live performance of **Annie Get Your Gun** with the entire sweaty but happy cast lined up to sing one last chorus of *No Business Like Show Business*.

The ode to entertainment is working out of this shared tradition; it may also be shown to us in such a way that, when the direct address comes, we're prepared for it. The change from third person to first person isn't perceived as a grammatical error (as it it is in a Godard film). In the first rendition of *That's Entertainment* from **The Band Wagon**, the ode is a plot-song with the representatives of high art trying to convince hoofer Astaire that all successful art is entertainment (even if it's based on **Faust**). We're on the stage of an empty theater with the first chorus shot from the observation point of a spectator also on the stage, the third-person perspective. Midway through the first chorus, Astaire buys the message; his participation in the rest of the number causes a sung scene (third person) to become a sung number (first person) as the action shifts to the performing apron of the stage and the point of view shifts to that of a spectator in the theater. But the theater is empty, and we the spectators are happy to fill the void. The audience in the film is even more spectral than usual, as

That's Entertainment switches from indirect ...

37

the effort to convince Astaire becomes a direct plea to us. *That's Entertainment* creates an informal proscenium as an arena for direct address to the spectator. We accept this convention, as we accept the message that all art is entertainment.

It can be argued that the ode to entertainment is the least-estranging form of direct address because it depends so much upon the internal audience and because its message carries the day. But direct address in the musical is not limited to the ode numbers. It is not even limited to the numbers. Within the world of the narrative, it is sometimes permissible for a character in the story to look directly into the lens and speak to the audience. That character, however, can't be just any old person, and certainly not a third-world radical. He is more likely to be that grand old man of the music hall, Maurice Chevalier. In **The Love Parade** (1929), **One Hour With You** (1932), **Love Me Tonight** (1932), and **The Lady Dances** (1934), which are operettas directed by Lubitsch and Mamoulian, Chevalier is permitted a glance at us even when there is no internal audience in sight. Early in **The Love Parade**, Chevalier plays a scene with a servant, picks up his trademark straw hat, proceeds out to the balcony, and performs directly to the camera his farewell to Paris. Suddenly the world is transformed into a music hall, the balcony into a stage. Were such a device inserted into a Godard film (and in fact Godard frequently has performers break into song as an estranging effect), it would no doubt wrench us from our immersion in the constructed flow of the narrative, especially since such a sequence would be radically at odds with the material surrounding it on either side. Lubitsch, however, quickly integrates the musical interlude back into the narrative by inserting reaction

Chevalier sings *I'm Glad I'm Not Young Any More* in **Gigi**

shots of women in balconies, women in windows, women in cafés all responding to Chevalier's charm.

By the time of **Gigi**, 1958, Chevalier's status as one of the last custodians of the live-entertainment tradition is so powerful that he may address an entire number, *I'm Glad I'm Not Young Any More*, to the spectator without even suggesting that he is really singing to an audience in the film. This song does indeed break out of the narrative world of the film; it is not Honoré but Chevalier himself for whom we feel such nostalgia. But the emotion itself and the tradition that evoked it cancel any critical tendencies toward that tradition. Chevalier rests totally within the entertainment tradition whereas Godard stands outside it and, ultimately, against it. It's absolutely essential to see a technique such as direct address in this historical context. Otherwise one may argue that direct address is inherently subversive or radical. It is not.

Direct address may just as well signify the intimacy of live entertainment. Or its alienating effect may cancel out. Two quite radical instances of direct address, radical in the sense of strongly disruptive to the narrative flow, seem to break the narrative only for the purpose of calling attention to an affirmation of entertainment which follows. The finale of **The Pirate** affirms illusionism; the *Dames* title number affirms voyeurism.

Near the end of **The Pirate** a huge close-up of Gene Kelly announces to us 'Ladies and Gentlemen, don't move, don't stir, the best is still to come'. The close-up is quite jarring, for many spectators may actually have thought the film was over; Kelly almost steps off the screen to call them back to their seats. Moreover, the cut to the close-up from the action preceding it breaks nearly every Hollywood rule for smooth transitions. The cut itself is more jarring than a dissolve would be. The sound does not carry over the cut; Kelly's voice starts abruptly on the close-up. The close-up is not matched for background with the preceding full shot; it is shot against a neutral black backdrop. This serves to take the close-up out of spatial and temporal continuity with the shot preceding and the dissolve following it. Kelly's facial expression does not match the full shot, nor does his head position match precisely. And the change in image size is extreme with only a slight change in angle, making of it a 'jump cut'.

All these transgressions make for an extremely abrupt and disorienting transition, far more so than in a similar transition at the end of **Take Me Out to the Ball Game** which uses both the dissolve and sound overlap, as well as a complete change in time and space (thus avoiding the jump) to ease the transition. The close-up is estranging in another sense, for it calls attention to the way musicals traditionally make us identify with the internal audience. Just which audience is Kelly addressing, we may ask: the audience which has witnessed Serafin's supposed last performance; the audience present at Kelly and Garland's *Be a Clown* which follows; or the audience present at both events, that is, the audience of the film, **The Pirate**? When we are encouraged to ask such questions, we are called away from our

40

immersion in the fiction, distanced in that we are asked to reflect upon the spectacle itself. But what we are asked to reflect upon is the tradition to which **The Pirate** belongs — that of the magic show, hocus-pocus, illusionism. The close-up calls our attention to the value of this tradition of which the film itself is a part, and the final number which Kelly beckons us to observe celebrates the fine art of being a clown. Direct address is indeed an 'alienation effect' in the Brechtian sense, but it does not 'alienate' us in the everyday sense of the term.

★ My discussion of *Dames* is indebted to Lucy Fischer, 'The Image of Woman as Image: the Optical Politics of *Dames*', **Film Quarterly**, vol. 30 (Fall 1976) pp.9-10.

Similarly in **Dames** we are presented with a spectacle which is self-conscious in a way only Busby Berkeley could be. The number **Dames** comes as part of the final, successful show which celebrates yet another victory of what might be termed the 'prurient' ethic over the 'Puritan' ethic. ★ Commencing at an all-male theatrical board meeting, the spectacle is framed by a debate as to which aspect of a show is most important to its (financial) success. Dick Powell has the answer: 'Tell the truth you go to see those beautiful dames', he sings to his fellow men. But through a cut similar to that which excluded the internal audience, the remark is addressed directly to us. Such an address forces the spectator to assume the persona of a lustful male at a girlie show; and the spectacle which follows rewards him.

The camera peeks at the dames in negligees, sleeping, bathing and dressing. But just as we are about to see the real thing, the

Berkeley 'givin' them what they want' in **Dames**

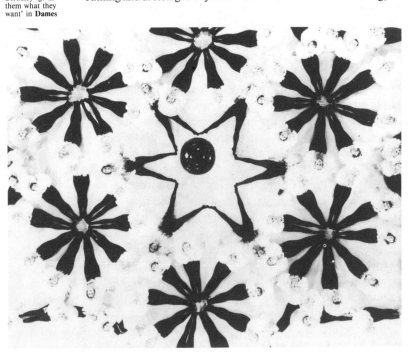

camera playfully withdraws as if punishing us for our desire. In one shot girls run up to the camera to conceal their naked bodies from its gaze. And of course we are treated to the typical Berkeley 'crotch shot' in which the camera travels down a row of girls spread-eagle on the floor as one by one their legs 'go down' for the phallic lens. But the spectator feels no real discomfort since his own voyeurism is transferred to the camera and his guilt absolved through the confession extracted from him by Dick Powell ('Tell the truth you go to see those beautiful dames'). The camera takes on the role of the internal audience as mediator of vision. A lot of the appeal of Berkeley's numbers in the days before he was considered an abstract expressionist must have centred on the glimpses the audience got at forbidden sexual pleasures. The *Dames* number seems to want to reassure us that the secrecy upon which cinematic voyeurism is based will always be protected by the camera's intervening eye. *Dames* asks us to give thanks to show business for the pleasures we are about to receive.

The World Backstage

Seemingly even more Brechtian than the use of direct address is the penchant the backstage musical has for revealing its own inner gears to the film audience. For as we have seen, we do not always take the view of the audience in the theater. Sometimes we get to go places where our counterpart live theater audience is proscribed, always during the narrative portions of the film but frequently during the shows as well. The shot from the theater's wings may represent just another interesting angle on the show, but even then it reveals the show's mechanics in the same shot as the show itself. Often the wings shot is a subjective-point-of-view shot in which one of the performers observes another, yet even then the subjective view from the wings demystifies the illusion a live show creates. Not only does it reveal the stage paraphernalia used to create the magic which the theatrical audience sees, but even more revealingly, it shows the performance as a routine, a job. In **Easter Parade,** for example, we see Astaire observing Garland's solo from the wings. Instead of enjoying the performance, he is observing the lack of audience response. Putting on a show is revealed as an act of audience manipulation when Astaire orders the stage manager to keep sending Garland flowers because 'it's good for business'. The shot from the wings may even reveal the production itself as an act of extreme calculation. Early in **The Band Wagon** we are shown Jeffrey Cordova as Oedipus Rex from the point of view of

Astaire in the wings. The camera is carefully positioned to reveal to us
Cordova's milking of the internal audience for applause. In yet
another act of demystification, the shot from the wings may contrast
the happy illusion onstage to a more grim reality backstage. In **Show
Boat** (1951) the scene of Julie's eviction in the wings is played in the
same frame as a cheerful production number on stage.

The demystifying shot is never used alone, however. It is
always cut in with shots from the point of view of the theatrical
audience, shots which mystify the performance. One can speak of a
pattern of demystification and remystification operating in the
filming of onstage numbers in backstage musicals. Complete
destruction of filmic illusion is impossible, of course, even in those
Godard films which show the camera in the frame, since this can only
be achieved by the camera photographing its reflection in a mirror.
The camera making the film cannot directly photograph itself
photographing the film. But there is an immense difference between
Godard's demystification and that of MGM, although, as with direct
address, the techniques used may be the same.

In modernist films remystification is an undesired by-
product, the fallout of demystification. Godard would show the
camera if only he could. But in the Hollywood musical, a new
mystification is the desired end result of demystification. In backstage
musicals and film-within-a-film musicals, two movements inevitably
take place. First, the making of entertainment is demystified; we are
taken into the world on the other side of the curtain, shown the
rehearsals. The aura of stars is reduced when we see them offstage as
'real people', especially in films such as **Sweethearts** and **The Barkleys**

43

of Broadway where legendary screen duos MacDonald and Eddy, Astaire and Rogers, play husband and wife teams who bicker incessantly behing the scenes. Most of the Warners' backstage musicals of the early 1930s show us rehearsals for numbers which later emerge as transcendant spectacles (for example, *Pettin' in the Park* in **Gold Diggers of 1933**). Late MGM musicals, especially those scripted by Betty Comden and Adolph Green (**The Barkleys of Broadway, The Band Wagon, Singin' in the Rain, It's Always Fair Weather, Bells Are Ringing**) delight in exposing as products of financial or emotional manipulation shows which represent 'wrong' kinds of entertainment. Shots from the wings in **Easter Parade** and **The Band Wagon** did not demystify the final, successful show. Rather, they exposed in the case of **The Band Wagon** pretentious elite art, and in the case of **Easter Parade** an attempt to force an elegant performance style upon a folksy comic persona (Garland). After the original shows convert to the correct style, we no longer see them from the wings; we see them from the mystifying point of view of the audience in the theater.

In this way demystification is always followed by a new mystification, the celebration of the seamless final show or placing back on her pedestal of a disgraced performer. No matter how much of the seamier side of entertainment has been exposed, it is always 'Mrs Norman Maine' by the end. Demystification splits open the narrative, exposes the world backstage, speaks in the first person. But the narrative gets sutured back together again for the final bow. It is unusual for a number to end on a demystifying shot. The preferred closing shot is a cut or dolly-in to a close-up of the performer, sealed into her third-person reality.

The wrong kind of show: the Faustian musical comedy in **The Band Wagon**

Technology revealed in **Singin' in the Rain**

And the World behind the Camera

Hollywood behind-the-scenes narratives would seem to be even more illusion-shattering than backstage musicals which attempt to pass their numbers off as live entertainment. Musicals about Hollywood almost always become musicals about making musicals. Two of the best-known musicals of the 1950s — **Singin' in the Rain** and **A Star is Born** — belong to this club, but behind-the-camera musicals have existed from the very beginning. ★ Even the least sophisticated of these films must, it seems, inevitably destroy the musical's heartfelt belief that musical movies are born of spontaneous combustion. The more sophisticated ones explicitly set out to destroy this illusion. By 1954, **A Star is Born** could even be cynical about two of Hollywood's most cherished myths: that movies materialize out of the air, and that movie stars are just as charming and glamorous offscreen as on. A few of these films center their efforts on the technology itself. In the most extreme cases, demystification appears total; the technology appears to take over the screen, in the process obscuring the performance itself. This would seem a blatant contradiction to the rule of folk art. But mystification always comes back and folk relations are restored. Either technology is revealed as a force performance can conquer, or the technology actually becomes the show.

    Show Girl in Hollywood seems to have been made (in 1930) to sing the praises of sound-on-disc recording rather than the girl herself. In an extraordinary sequence in which we see a large production number being shot for the film-within-a-film, **Show Girl** becomes almost documentary in its efforts to show the new

★ Examples include **Married in Hollywood** (1929), **The Talk of Hollywood** (1930), **Show Girl in Hollywood** (1930), **Easy Go** (1930), **Anchors Aweigh** (1944), **On an Island With You** (1948), **Singin' in the Rain** (1952), **A Star is Born** (1954), and **Silk Stockings** (1956).

technology to the spectator. In the opening shot, a curtain parts to reveal not the expected proscenium stage but rather a movie set. After we recover our bearings, we realize we are looking onto the reverse angle of the anticipated shot, that is to say, over the footlights of the internal proscenium onto the crew for the shooting of the show within the film within the film (called 'Rainbow Girl'). To be sure the curtain has opened on a show, but the show is the making of a Hollywood musical; the disorienting cut calls attention to this reversal of the usual procedure. Soon the impression that the making of the film *is* the show intensifies as we see it shot in so fragmented a manner that we could not possibly be entertained by the performance alone. Of the many camera positions, most are demystifying; few show the number as transparent spectacle. Many reveal all or part of the movie set on which the number is being shot. Several times the montage returns to the shot of the film crew and equipment from behind the footlights, a position which doesn't show the number at all. Even more demystifying are shots from inside the camera-muffling booth. The camera shooting the number occupies a prominent position in the foreground of our frame as we view the camera and its operator in silhouette with the number itself in the far background. And on the sound track we hear not just the silly song being performed but also the camera noise, subjective from inside the booth. The number concludes with shots of technicians monitoring the sound and men making Vitaphone discs of the performance. Throughout this rhythmic montage, the performance itself is either distanced or displaced completely. Such a technological education, while demystifying in a literal sense, becomes mystifying at the level of audience impact, as we see film technology as a new form of spectacle, a new show.

Show Girl in Hollywood is unable to take the ironic distance from 'Rainbow Girl' that **Singin' in the Rain** twenty years later takes from 'The Dancing Cavalier', its early talkie musical within the film. An entire number in **Singin' in the Rain** is built around the looping of Kathy Selden's voice for Lina Lamont's. Once again the technology seems to become the show. Yet **Singin' in the Rain** ultimately denies that technology is responsible for our pleasure. *You Were Meant For Me*, the romantic number on the deserted sound stage between Gene Kelly and Debbie Reynolds, demystifies only in order to restore illusion. Although Kelly gives us a look at the hardware behind movie magic (the wind machine, the soft lights) in an introduction to the song, the camera arcs around and comes in for a tighter shot of the couple during the central portion of the number, reframing to exclude the previously exposed equipment. We regress from an exposé of romantic duets to an example of a romantic duet, which, along with all the others, lies about its past. The early talkie musical may be a product of a show of technology but **Singin' in the Rain** remains, rhetorically at least, the product of magic. It's as if we've been given a complete confession in order to conceal the real crime. For what's mystified in the end is the origin of the musical film itself. The behind-the-camera musical ultimately denies that technological calculation lies behind the Hollywood musical's most endearing charms.

Conclusion

At first glance the Hollywood musical seems to be an exception to descriptions of the 'classical' film which always tries to conceal its own workings. The musical appears to be constantly breaking through its own glossy surface, more like a modernist film is supposed to do. Apparently this model for 'classical' narrative is unable to account for a reflexive but conservative form such as the musical in which each modernist creation is also a cancellation. The proscenium creates distance so that we can watch distance being bridged. The audience in the film stands between us and the performance in order to make us identify even more closely with the experience of live theater. Direct address pierces the narrative enclosure in order to affirm the tradition of entertainment whose story the film is telling us. And technology is exposed within the films to set us up for an ultimate mystification of the Hollywood musical itself. Unless we put the Hollywood musical in its proper place in the history of entertainment, we may mistake it for a modernist film, or, worse, we may never see what its revelations are trying to conceal.

A publicity still
from **Babes in Arms**
contrasts swing's
dynamism with
opera's static
quality

3:

The Celebration of Popular Song

We have seen that the Hollywood musical wished to identify itself with live-entertainment practices more directly audience-involving and with economic relations less alienating. As a reflexive form, the musical is able to use the narrative portions of the film to signal the numbers. The Hollywood musical's innate reflexivity may then be used to glorify its own musical form, identifying that form with folk relations. The chief instrument for the privileging of popular song is the song lyric itself. We are all aware that popular songs of the pre-rock era dealt primarily with the moon and June. But it is necessary to remember that the primary rhyme for 'moon' and 'June' was 'croon'.

The Reflexive Song Lyric

If you are . . . doing **An American in Paris** *and you're talking about a girl and you're saying that she's wonderful, you sing 's'wonderful, s'marvelous, she should care for me'. You're telling the other fellow about it; you state the thesis, you state the idea, then you further it in dance form. 'Singin' in the rain', you say, 'I'm singin' in the rain, just singin' in the rain. What a marvelous feeling. I'm happy again.' You state it; now you prove it. You further your thesis by dancing it. ★*

★ Gene Kelly,
quoted in
The Magic Factory,
p.54

We're trying to tell a story with music and song and dance and not just with words. For instance, if the boy tells a girl that he loves her, he doesn't just say it, he sings it. ★

★ Gene Kelly
in **Summer Stock**

49

By the 1950s the word was out in Hollywood that everything in the musical had to be conveyed in musical terms. If, in the Western, the bad guy must wear a black hat, then in the musical the bad guy will be hostile to jazz or perform in the wrong musical style. Ginger Rogers in **Swing Time** could never find true love with a Latin band leader, nor could Cyd Charisse in **The Band Wagon** really love a ballet choreographer. Sometimes the bad girl in musicals can't sing at all; in **Blues in the Night,** she sings off key; in **Singin' in the Rain** Lina Lamont has to borrow somebody else's voice. When a straight film was remade as a musical its plot and setting had to be adapted to accommodate not only the placement of songs but also this basic musical vocabulary.

When **The Shop Around the Corner** becomes **In the Good Old Summertime**, the leather-goods store becomes a sheet-music store so that Margaret Sullavan's ability to sell becomes Judy Garland's ability to 'sell a song'. In the musical remake of **A Star is Born** (1954) the actress becomes a musical-comedy star based on Judy Garland herself. In **Silk Stockings**, Ninotchka's satire on the Puritanism of the Communists is transformed into Ninotchka's marked hostility to the spirit of musical entertainment. And in **High Society**, the musical version of **The Philadelphia Story**, the territory of the 'rich and mighty' is transferred to Newport, symbol both of immense wealth and of the spirit of jazz, elements which merge in Louis Armstrong's final jazz trumpet version of **The Wedding March**.

Numbers in which a performer sings and dances *as* he sings about singing and dancing abound in the musical film. Some, like Gene Kelly's 'singin' and dancin' in the rain', have passed into legend. Kelly's alphabet consists of song and dance, but so does his meaning. We might call *Singin' in the Rain* a reflexive song. One need only glance over the titles of songs performed in Fred Astaire musicals to see how frequently the reflexive song lyric shows up in the musical film: *Music Makes Me, Cheek to Cheek, Let's Face the Music and Dance, Let Yourself Go, Never Gonna Dance, I Won't Dance, Shall We Dance, Change Partners, Dream Dancing, You're So Easy to Dance With, A Couple of Song and Dance Men, It Only Happens When I Dance with You, Steppin Out with My Baby, Shoes with Wings On, I Wanna Be a Dancin' Man, Shine on Your Shoes.* And this list does not include dance-name songs such as the Carioca, the Continental, the Piccolino, the Yam, and the Sluefoot, nor does it include the many other Astaire songs whose *lyrics* refer primarily or incidentally to song or dance.

The reflexive song lyric celebrating the power of music (or the power of popular entertainment in general) came to be institutionalized at MGM. Much of this material was 'house composed' sometimes employing producer Arthur Freed or his associate Roger Edens as lyricist, sometimes borrowing reflexive song lyrics from Broadway shows or Tin Pan Alley. Arthur Freed had been a popular lyricist before becoming the major producer of Hollywood musicals. As lyricist, he was responsible for the reflexive songs *Singin' in the Rain, Broadway Rhythm* and *Broadway Melody,* all written for MGM musicals of the 1920s and 1930s. When Freed became a producer in the 1940s, he was able to recycle his own reflexive songs; all three of the songs just mentioned were used in **Singin' in the Rain**. MGM had employed Freed's lyrics in the studio's **Broadway Melody** series (1929, 1936, 1938, 1940). Each backstage musical in this series would include a new *Ode to Broadway*, usually placed in the finale as part of the celebration of entertainment represented by the final show. The *Broadway Melody* theme was repeated in each new edition, with the addition of *Broadway Rhythm* (for the 1938 edition) and *Please Don't Monkey with Broadway* (for the 1940 **Broadway Melody**). The staging of *Your Broadway and My Broadway* was typical, featuring Sophie Tucker and full chorus in a nostalgic tribute to entertainment. **Singin' in the Rain**'s *Broadway Ballet* continued this tradition through parody. Reflexive song lyrics were used and re-used; their message was heard over and over again.

Redefining Music as Song

Where there's music, there'll be singing
Where there's singing you'll find skies of blue
For when all the world goes wrong
a simple little song
will always bring a rainbow smiling through
With a rainbow, there'll be laughter
Chasing after sunshine from above.
Where there's sunshine, there'll be music
And where there's music there's love.

Where There's Music introduces a medley of old standards Judy Garland sings in the final show of **Presenting Lily Mars**. Connections between music and love are often expressed through reflexive song lyrics but rarely in so obvious a causal chain as in this Roger Edens lyric. The lyric is instructive not because it's poetically rich but because it's so skeletal. What is most instructive about this entirely conventional reflexive song lyric is that, in order to link music and love, it must first *redefine music as singing*. In order to sing the praises of music, the general term 'music' must be particularized as 'song'. The redefinition masks the lack of a real equivalence between the two terms. 'Where there's music, there'll be singing', says the lyric, conveniently ignoring the fact that song is a hybrid form of presentation, combining the purely symbolic 'language' of music with the referential language of words in order to achieve a synthesis which is also referential and which may be addressed to an audience. Reflexive song lyrics make use of the verbal, referential part of a song to refer to the notion of singing itself. Without the words, music has trouble talking about itself. When MGM made the Strauss biopic, **The Great Waltz**, Oscar Hammerstein was commissioned to provide lyrics for the Strauss waltzes, transforming the waltz king into a song-writer. Only through the addition of lyrics could Strauss's life be material for the book of a musical and his waltzes material for love songs.

In privileging song over non-representational music, however, the Hollywood musical is not necessarily contrasting two languages (music and words) even when it seems to be doing so. Take, for example, another Roger Edens lyric, ★ *Music is Better than Words* from **It's Always Fair Weather**:

> Music *is better than words*
> *You break the spell when you start to speak*
> *That technique is all wrong.*
> *So forget about words and sing her a* song.

> [Emphasis by Jane Feuer]

★ Hugh Fordin, in The World of Entertainment (Garden City, NY: Doubleday, 1975) p.435, claims that Roger Edens was the actual lyricist for *Music is Better than Words,* officially credited to Betty Comden and Adolph Green. One can note the influence of Edens, Arthur Freed's associate producer, on Judy Garland's opera *vs* jazz special material.

In the very act of privileging the non-representational language of music over the representational language of words, a switch is made so that what at first seems to be a contrast between modes of representation actually becomes a contrast between modes of *presentation*. Instead of privileging music over words, the lyric actually privileges song over speech, that is sung words over spoken words. Remember Gene Kelly's pronouncement: 'he doesn't just say it, he sings it'.

What the musical can do that 'third-person' forms (such as narrative films and classical music) can't do, according to this line of reasoning, is to show the process of a transformation from one mode of presentation to another. In becoming song, language is in a sense transfigured, lifted up into a higher, more expressive realm. No better example of such a transformation exists than the very sequence in **Summer Stock** from which Kelly's speech is taken. In a dialogue sequence preceding the number, Kelly extols the virtues of theater, illusionism, and 'hokum' to Garland's naive farmer. Although the dialogue scene is reflexive in content, it is filmed as a self-contained finished sequence, not as an address to the spectator. The camera tracks in onto Garland over Kelly, giving us a closer view onto the scene but also putting us in the position of eavesdropping on the conversation. The spectator is a voyeur, not a participant in the reflexive scene.

As Kelly explains that a love scene must be sung, words fail him, and he begins to demonstrate. At this point, as in *That's Entertainment,* a closed story is transformed into direct address through the agency of the musical number itself. Kelly's speech slides into song. The action moves to the performing part of the stage. Spotlights come up on Garland and Kelly. And the spectator is no longer looking at an airtight, self-contained chronicle. The scene of explanation of the need for direct address becomes instead a demonstration of its potency, as Kelly and Garland face the camera and perform *You Wonderful You* all for us.

By redefining music as song, reflexive song lyrics venerate a way of singing specific to American popular music in general and to musical comedy in particular. Music critic Henry Pleasants speaks of the popular singer's acceptance of song as a 'lyrical extension of speech'. ★ In musical comedy ordinary speech and music are linked each time a song is born out of a scene of spoken dialogue. In favoring song as a mode of presentation, the musical champions as well its own first-person mode. This is the function of the reflexive song lyric for the rhetoric of the genre as a whole.

The musical celebrates its own kind of music — what I have been calling popular music. Both within and without the musical film, there exists some confusion as to what this term means and which music it refers to. Part of the problem is that for a period of time roughly coinciding with the heyday of the Hollywood musical, the so-called 'Swing Era' (*c.*1935-55), popular music in America was very closely related to jazz. Henry Pleasants reminds us that certain elements are in fact common to all American popular music:

> *a steady, swinging, propulsive beat, supporting a rhythmically free, more or less improvisational melody, the basic melodic material being the popular song.* ★

Jazz critic Martin Williams follows Pleasants in pointing to the many affinities between jazz and popular music:

> *It is not surprising that all American popular music, and some American concert music as well, were once commonly referred to as 'jazz', because the influence of jazz and of pre-jazz Afro-American music is everywhere in our musical life — on Broadway, in musical films, in the hotel dance band, in the 'hit parade', in the concert hall. . . so apparently 'square' a popular song as* Dancing in the Dark *would not have been written without the powerful and pervasive effect of the musical force we call 'jazz'.* ★ ★

★ The Great American Popular Singers, p.35

★ 'What is this Thing Called Jazz?' in **Jam Session,** ed. Ralph Gleason (New York: G.P.Putnam, 1958) p.182

★ ★ Where's the Melody? (New York: Minerva Press, 1961) pp.x-xi

53

Nevertheless for the purpose of the musical film, jazz possessed two traits show music did not possess to the same degree: an (Afro-American) ethnic folk origin, and a high degree of improvisation. That is, jazz may be identified as a *folk* music and as a *spontaneous* music. Hall and Whannel are somewhat more detailed in listing those 'folk elements' jazz has retained as it became a popular music and, ultimately, an elite music.

1. simplicity of form (relative to European music)
2. a tone that expressed the personality of the player not the classical ideal of purity of tone
3. a core of professionals surrounded by a number of semi-professionals and amateurs
4. 'improvisation and spontaneity are still paramount'
5. surrounded by a relaxed and informal atmosphere: 'the best jazz is still night-club or "jam session" jazz'. ★

★ Hall and Whannel, **The Popular Arts,** pp.72-3

It is no coincidence that these are the same 'folk' qualities the musical film wishes to retain: the direct mode of presentation, the amateur quality, spontaneity and informality. By calling its own music 'jazz' the musical film was able to profit rhetorically from its immersion in the Swing Era confusion over terminology. The musical could claim for its own the folk roots and spontaneous quality of jazz. Then it could use 'jazz' to cancel out more elite, European kinds of music — opera, for instance.

Opera *vs* Jazz:
The Theme of Popular *vs* Elite Art

In the Hollywood musical, the war between elite and popular art came to be represented by a standard plot which I will call the 'opera *vs* swing' narrative. Just as in **The Jazz Singer**, a conflict between generations is expressed in a clash between mammy singing ('jazz') and Kol Nidre (traditional religious music), so the opera *vs* swing plot typically involves a son who wants to sing swing and a father or matriarchal grandmother figure who prefers classical musicianship. As in **The Jazz Singer** the plot is resolved by reconciling the generations through a merger of musical styles. In both cases jazz represents a 'folk' music which is nevertheless not a traditional music; it always represents the music of the future, the promise of youth.

Broadly speaking, the traditional music *vs* jazz plot is as old as the genre itself. But opera *vs* swing plots caught on big in a series of musicals produced by Joe Pasternak at MGM in the 1940s. Through these MGM musicals, Pasternak was able to continue a tradition — begun with the Deanna Durbin films he produced at Universal in the

1930s — of introducing concert music and classical musicans into the film musical. Of course neither the plot structure nor the notion of setting opera and jazz in conflict was invented by Pasternak. The preference for jazz reflects commonly held biases of the mass audience; the plot structure is part of the basic syntax of the genre. The battle between popular and elite art was waged on every front in the Hollywood musical. One can see it in the confrontation of operatic and music-hall vocal styles that always symbolized the sexual struggle of Maurice Chevalier and Jeanette MacDonald in their Paramount operettas of the late 1920s and early 1930s. Ballet and tap dancing went to war throughout the musical's lifespan. In **Easy Go** (1930), Buster Keaton parodies ballet in a film-within-the-film. **Shall We Dance** in 1937 has Fred Astaire playing a ballet star who secretly wants to tap. For the 1938 **Goldwyn Follies**, George Balanchine himself choreographed a ballet in which two families feuded over their respective tastes for ballet and tap dancing. **The Band Wagon** in 1953 proved tap's superiority as ballerina Cyd Charisse learned to click her heels. In the 1960s, **Bye Bye Birdie** had the Russian ballet quite literally speeded up in order to make way for the popular music of the times — Elvis Presley style rock 'n' roll. The present decade proves no exception to the popular/elite rule. 1980's **Fame** gives us an update on the classical *vs* jazz, youth *vs* age dilemma when a young man forced against his will to study violin literally blows a fuse with his beloved electronic synthesizer during a classical string-ensemble rehearsal.

Classical music, popular music, ballet and tap dancing may be said to be elements of the genre's vocabulary. The particular syntax opposing popular and elite elements arises out of the genre's overall rhetoric of affirming itself by applauding popular forms. When classical music comes to be used in a Hollywood musical (which by definition already contains popular music) the logic of the genre, which always uses cultural prejudices to its own benefit, dictates the war of musical styles. Classical music or ballet may remain merely a replacement for popular music. Many Pasternak films featured singers with operatic voices (Deanna Durbin, Kathryn Grayson); symphony orchestras and conductors (Leopold Stokowski and José Iturbi); or classical musicians as heroes (June Allyson as a pregnant bass player in **Music for Millions**). Oscar Levant's classical piano interludes in Freed Unit musicals didn't always imply a parody of elite music.

Those musicals which do raise the classical/popular conflict to a central position in the film's plot always show the triumphant victory of the popular style. **It Happened in Brooklyn** (MGM, Cummings Unit), **This Time for Keeps** (MGM, Pasternak Unit), and **The Time, the Place and the Girl** (Warners), all released in 1946-7, show opera singing or symphonic conducting assimilated to a popular style. In the latter two films, the comic plot is resolved when the recalcitrant father or grandad figure converts to the joys of swing. **The Time, the Place and the Girl** celebrates victory when the conductor grandfather jams with a jazz band at a party given for the opening of a Broadway show. **This Time for Keeps** has the opera-singing father (Lauritz Melchior) reprise *Easy to Love* previously used twice in popular contexts. In neither film is there any actual hostility to classical music; rather classical music is seen as lacking a potency which may only be gained by a conversion to popular music. **It Happened in Brooklyn** works by expressing this generalized sense of castration in terms of a more specific (sexual) notion of castration. Full of thinly veiled sexual metaphors, the film plays upon a widespread cultural association between popular music and sexual potency. Although such an association is most often remembered in connection with the pelvis of Elvis Presley, it actually dates back much further in the history of popular music. The very term 'jazz', frequently used as a generic term for all popular music, originally possessed a vulgar sexual meaning. **It Happened in Brooklyn** uses the association between popular music and sexual plenitude to define classical music as a castrated form of popular music.

Brooklyn, as that province of New York City providing a locus for popular music, is opposed to Europe whose music represents a no-longer-vital tradition. The classical side is represented by Peter Lawford as an emotionally repressed British classical musician and by Kathryn Grayson as an operatically trained music teacher who fears that her voice is 'too cold'. As Lawford so eloquently puts it in the film, 'what's missing in my music is what's missing in me'. Lawford's grandfather, who becomes a catalyst for the forces of swing, explains to Sinatra that Lawford's music 'isn't young. Everything he writes sounds like a funeral march.' Once again classical music is defined by what it 'isn't' (and by what swing *is*). It is up to the representatives of Brooklyn, Frank Sinatra and Jimmy Durante, to teach Lawford to 'swing' and ultimately to match him with his musical correlative (Grayson) by bringing him to Brooklyn.

An exchange between Sinatra and Lawford early in the film illustrates the way Lawford's inadequacies as a man are paired with the inadequacies of his preferred musical idiom. Lawford is seated at the piano, playing a classical piece; Sinatra shows him how to 'swing' in the form of the number *Whose Baby Are You?* When Lawford remarks that the number sounds like Mendelssohn's *Italian Symphony,* Sinatra responds, 'sure the *notes* are the same but it hasn't got a beat'. The endearing philistinism of this remark should not be allowed to eclipse its significance. European music is seen as decrepit, cold, out of touch with the needs of the people; whereas swing, as the music of the folk of Brooklyn, represents youth, community, warmth, personal expression and spontaneity; in short, all those 'folk' qualities most prized by the Hollywood musical. As Jimmy Durante puts it in one of his pro-vaudeville routines in the film: 'It doesn't matter what you sing, the song's gotta come from the heart.' But the point seems to be that only swing music does come from the heart. Only swing music flows directly from the popular entertainer to the spectator. Lawford's composition is not brought to life until Sinatra sets words to it and it becomes the popular ballad *Time After Time.* Once again, 'classical' music is transformed into swing.

The Judy Garland Opera *vs* Swing Number

In the 1930s, RKO showed a preference for jazz over ballet by identifying jazz dance with its leading dancing star, Fred Astaire. In the 1940s, MGM privileged the same swing music by identifying it with the studio's biggest singing star, Judy Garland. Conversely one could argue that both Garland's and Astaire's fortunes were enhanced by an association with the most popular musical styles of the times. Judy Garland's emergence coincides with both the heyday of the swing era — the late 1930s and the war years — and the emergence of the Freed Unit at MGM. Nowhere was the association of swing with youth and energy more apparent than in the Mickey Rooney - Judy Garland co-starring films of this period. One thinks in particular of *The La Conga* (*sic*) number in **Strike Up the Band** (1940), in which the energy level of the youthful co-stars threatens to make their eyes pop out of their heads. In this early stage of her career, Judy Garland nearly always (with the exception of **The Wizard of Oz**) played the cheerful, spirited adolescent who liked to sing swing. Looking at Judy Garland musicals from this period, one finds an opera *vs* swing number in nearly every film.

Garland's first MGM role was in a two-reeler, **Every Sunday** (1936), which pitted Judy against another young MGM contract player who had an operatic voice — Deanna Durbin. The opera/jazz conflict was at the center of the conception for the girls' first film. Roger Edens seized upon this precedent in arranging numbers for subsequent Judy Garland musicals. *Opera vs Jazz* from **Babes in Arms** and *Tom, Tom the Piper's Son* from **Presenting Lily Mars** show swing music replacing or overtaking classical music. Judy Garland's contribution to the all-star musical **Thousands Cheer** has an Edens lyric contrasting Tin Pan Alley and Carnegie Hall. Also in **Presenting Lily Mars** is a number which satirizes elite art, the third major way musicals prove the superiority of swing.

Opera vs Jazz, from **Babes in Arms**, takes the form of a musical 'duel' between Garland and another young singer with an operatic voice, Betty Jaynes. Performed on request at a party where the older generation of vaudeville performers and their children have gathered, the number consists of a recitative duet followed by a singing competition. The structure of the verse as well as the way the number is shot and the way the girls gesture within the frame points to an extreme similarity as they sing together 'To look at us you'd never dream the two of us are twins'. Garland takes up the recital which stresses the similarity in matters of taste between the 'twins', a parallelism emphasized by verse structure and musical structure: 'we both like to sing and we both like to dance', for instance. In fact, 'our tastes are just the same except for just one thing'; 'I like opera' (Jaynes) and 'I like swing' (Garland). Another chorus highlights more similarities, this time sung in duet and ending with the parallel lyrics 'I sing sweet' and 'I sing hot'. 'I sing sweet' is sung 'sweet', i.e. operatically, but 'I sing hot' is 'growled'. At this point Garland yields to Jaynes who performs an operatic arrangement of *You Are My Lucky Star* complete with ornamentation which completely overloads the familiar Freed-Brown pop tune. In yet another precise parallel, Garland does a swing number about the Barber of Seville with lyrics that parody opera characters. Garland is accompanied by the multi-talented Mickey Rooney, slapping a bass; the swing number is delivered with characteristic intensity, energy and movement. A musical 'duel' follows in which the girls duet in their respective styles to another Freed-Brown ditty – *Broadway Rhythm*, the by-then-standard hymn to the contagious energy of the Great White Way ('Broadway rhythm it's got me, everybody sing and dance'). During this rendition, Judy and Mickey dance while the opera singer remains stiff and stationary. But the number ends with both girls swinging and snapping their fingers to the beat, representing yet another victory for swing. If both singing styles are supposed to be equally valid, as the verse seems to imply, then the choice of material for the body of the number is curious indeed. The opera singer is forced to do inappropriate arrangements of decidedly non-operatic material (Freed-Brown songs from earlier MGM musicals), the second of which is an ode to Broadway (not exactly the mecca of opera). Garland, on the other hand, gets to sing a 'swinging' arrangement of a number which parodies opera, plus the ode to Broadway, to which she 'swings' physically and to which dynamism is added by the camera's moving on its axis to accommodate Garland's movement. The strategy of the number consists in strongly implying that a difference in musical idiom is *significant,* then demonstrating swing's superiority. Swing is contagious and Jaynes catches it.

Other musicals repeat the motif of jazz overpowering classical music. **Murder at the Vanities**, a backstage-musical murder mystery, has members of Duke Ellington's orchestra literally pop up out of a concert orchestra to play a few blasts of jazz. The jazz eventually overtakes the classical. Jimmy Durante in **Music for Millions** turns a symphony rehearsal into a jam session. Starting with one trumpet blowing a jazz riff, the number spreads to the point where the entire orchestra is playing swing.

Sometimes swing overrides not classical music but rather traditional folk music, as in the *Portland Fancy* sequence in **Summer Stock**. The Portland Fancy is a traditional square dance performed by the stodgy Wingate Falls Historical Society. The Portland Fancy is presented as 'historic' in every way. A high-angle shot emphasizes the patterned, formal quality of the dance. The chorus kids from the show sprawl about, bored, in the lofts of the barn where the dance takes place. But then a transformation occurs, impelled by a change from spectator to participant on the part of the kids. One of them takes over the drums as the trumpet announces the change with a jazzy bugle call. The music shifts into swing time altering the melody of the Portland Fancy into an almost unrecognizable swing arrangement. Couples of chorus kids jitterbug in the center of the circle while the square dance continues around the edges. But the square dancers are now out of tempo with the swing music and have trouble keeping step. The staid, patterned composition of the traditional dance is broken by the jitterbuggers to the point where another high-angle shot reveals total chaos on the dance floor. Meanwhile, Gene Kelly breaks out of the square-dance formation to do a series of 'challenge' steps to which Garland eventually succumbs. *The Portland Fancy* finally becomes a 'hot' number addressed to the viewer, with the kids acting as the internal audience.

The *Portland Fancy* carefully shows us jazz cancelling traditional folk music. We keep the music of the Portland Fancy but change the arrangement. We keep the dance formation but change the type of steps and raise the energy level. Extending this pattern to the genre as a whole, it's possible to see precisely the same relationship operating between traditional folk music and jazz folk music. Jazz retains the folk aspects of the older music but dispenses with the old-fashioned aspects. It transforms a folk music which is historic to one which is alive. Swing speaks to the current generation. In **The Glenn Miller Story**, Miller changes a military marching tune into the *St Louis Blues* in swing time, and the men's step takes on bounce, rhythm and vitality. A general praises Miller for 'giving the men the music they like'. Of course, the music people like is always the currently popular form of music.

The Popularizing of Classical Music

Since people like popular music, they might be led to like classical music too if it is given the quality of dialogue, that is, if it is transformed into popular music. This seems to be the strategy underlying many of the Pasternak musicals. *The Joint is Really Jumping Down at Carnegie Hall,* Garland's number in **Thousands Cheer,** is accompanied by concert pianist José Iturbi playing boogie-woogie piano. Showing long-haired Iturbi performing in a popular style tends to humanize and popularize the classical musician as does pairing him with child stars: Deanna Durbin and Leopold Stokowski in **One Hundred Men and a Girl**; Margaret O'Brien and Iturbi in **Music for Millions.** Playing boogie woogie lends a new life and vigor to Iturbi's classical musicianship, just as, in **Shall We Dance,** Astaire puts taps on his ballet shoes to make ballet dancing more fun. The classical presence elevates the status of popular music just as jazz imbues concert music with humanizing folk qualities.

Both in the film musical and in the popular imagination, George Gershwin has become the prototype of an artist who managed to merge the popular qualities of a jazz idiom with the status, respectability and lasting quality of elite art. Although Gershwin died in 1937, his influence on the Hollywood musical continued to be felt.

In addition to the prodigious use of Gershwin's popular songs, his concert music, often performed by Oscar Levant, is featured in film musicals to a greater extent that that of any other composer with the possible exception of Tchaikovsky (a figure not unlike Gershwin in representing a combination of respectability and popularity). Implied or actual references to Gershwin are made in several musicals (other than those that would naturally occur in the Gershwin biopic). In **Lady Be Good** a lyric contains the words:

> *My lyrics aren't in a class with Ira Gershwin*
> *From Ira Gershwin I've lots to learn*

and

> *I'd bring out the Kern in you*
> *And you'd bring out the Gershwin in me.*

The lyric implicitly draws a parallel between the Gershwin brothers and the husband and wife song-writing team in the film, a parallel abetted by the use of the Gershwin title (**Lady Be Good**), interpolated songs, and an implied criticism of popular composers who forsake their true calling for the concert stage. Fred Astaire's character in **Shall We Dance** — the great Petrov, star of the Russian ballet who is really Pete Peters from Philadelphia — seems to be based on Gershwin. Such a character represents the successful combination of popular and elite musical forms: concert music and popular song in Gershwin's case; ballet and tap in Petrov's. The fact that Gershwin wrote the score for **Shall We Dance** further emphasizes the parallels between him and Astaire/Petrov. Musical 'cues' are employed to emphasize the relationship even more; the main theme from *Rhapsody in Blue* is played under Gershwin's name in the film's credits. The 'walking' bass jazz figure composed by Gershwin for Astaire's and Rogers' *Walking the Dog* routine on the ship's deck echoes the *Rhapsody* as well. Repeatedly the film reminds its audience that Gershwin was the man who actually did what Astaire wants to do in the film, to bring a revitalizing jazz influence to classical music.

The Gershwin example illuminates a number such as *The Joint is Really Jumping* in that it reveals the ambiguity surrounding an apparent desire to humanize and popularize classical music and musicians by including their most commercial representatives in the musical film. In a sense the classical music featured in the Hollywood musical is already popular: although Oscar Levant studied with Schoenberg, MGM does not include a twelve-tone piece in **An American in Paris**. Yet even though Tchaikovsky is already the most commercial of classical composers, and even though he employed Russian folk-musical material, he is unable to represent one key aspect of the Gershwin persona: an association with *jazz*. In short, some concert music may be popular, but it no longer represents a living tradition as Gershwin does and as swing does. The need to elevate Gershwin and the need to humanize Iturbi is connected to this perceived lack in the popular concert repertoire. Even when **The Band Wagon** proclaims that any kind of art is good so long as it is 'entertaining', there is still an implication that elite art (ballet and **Faust**) lacks qualities which only jazz can lend to it. The reverse is never so heavily stressed. Thus the finale of the successful show within **The Band Wagon** is *The Girl Hunt*, a *jazz* ballet. As with *Opera vs Jazz* from **Babes in Arms,** and the finale of **Shall We Dance,** the musical film emphasizes what popular art can contribute to elite art, even while trying to affirm the kind of status and longevity elite art can lend to the musical film.

Another opera *vs* jazz number from **Presenting Lily Mars** takes a satirical look at high art, an attitude pervading the Hollywood musical long before Comden and Green raised it to a thematic level. In the film, Lily Mars, an Indiana girl trying her big break on Broadway, vies with a sophisticated operetta singer for the love of a Broadway producer. Following a love ballad (called, typically, *I Hear Lovely Music*) sung by the operetta star to the producer at his apartment, the film cuts to a night-club sequence in which Lily sings with the Bob Crosby Big Band. Her number, however, is the same tune we have just heard the operetta star perform. Moreover, Lily does a parody chorus of the song in the form of an exaggerated mimicry of the other woman's pretentious operatic-singing style. Plots and numbers mimicking elite art or satirizing it indirectly permeate the Hollywood musical. As late as **Funny Girl** (1968), Barbra Streisand's burlesque version of Fanny Brice in Swan Lake rests firmly within this tradition. And as early as **The Broadway Melody** (1929), the first original MGM musical and the prototype for the backstage sub-genre, we are shown a fight between the conductor and the director over whether the music for the show should be played in highbrow or lowbrow fashion.

Almost every popular musical performance in **The Band Wagon** is matched up with a segment which parodies the lack of spontaneity and pretentiousness of the high-art world. Tony drops Gaby while attempting a ballet lift during a rehearsal of the pretentious Faustian *Band Wagon,* but in the *Girl Hunt* jazz ballet he lifts her effortlessly. The couple's relaxed offstage rehearsal of a dance to *You and the Night and the Music* literally explodes onstage at the dress rehearsal. Satire of the Faustian version of the show is achieved in part through so subtle a device as the musical arrangements associated with each version of the show. The music under the rehearsal segment in which Tony drops Gaby is a sedate balletic arrangement of *New Sun in the Sky* which becomes the first number in

Fanny Brice does
Swan Lake in
Funny Girl

the final show. This time, however, the song is given an upbeat, jazzy
tempo and instrumentation as part of a rousing production number of
Cyd Charisse and chorus; the affirmative lyric to the song with its
many images of rejuvenation and renewal is featured as well:
'Yesterday my heart sang a blue song, but today hear it hum a cheery

New Sun in the Sky
in **The Band Wagon**

new song.' The comic mishaps associated with *You and the Night and the Music* in dress rehearsal are emphasized by the heavy, overly orchestrated accompaniment as opposed to the simple piano accompaniment we heard at the unofficial rehearsal.

The entire sub-plot of **Silk Stockings** ridicules elite art through a farcical contrast between modern serious music and modern popular music. In fact, **Silk Stockings** scores its comic points through a remarkable comprehension of the by-then-well-entrenched pop/elite operation in Hollywood musicals. The plot concerns a Russian composer who has defected to Paris to write a score for a Hollywood film version of **War and Peace** produced by Steven Canfield (Astaire) and starring an Esther Williams character named Peggy Dayton. Since Peggy has never appeared in a non-musical and since she finds the Russian's music 'lousy', **War and Peace** is scrapped in favor of a vulgar musical saga of Napoleon and Josephine to be called 'Not Tonight'. As in **Singin' in the Rain**, the film within the film is remade as a musical. In the process, Boroff's famous serious composition *Ode to a Tractor* is mutilated when an American lyricist is hired to add words to some melodies from the ode.

In the debate surrounding this transformation within the film, we seem to get an apology for many of the customs of the Freed Unit itself. Peggy argues that Boroff is 'too square' whereas Canfield counters that he will 'lend prestige to the picture', just as presumably the inclusion of concert music lent prestige to MGM musicals. In fact, the example Astaire uses to prove his point in the film — the way in which a Tchaikovsky theme became the popular song *Our Love is Like a Melody* — bears an uncanny resemblance to the Sinatra-Iturbi debate in **Anchors Aweigh**. As Astaire says in **Silk Stockings**, 'In America we do this sort of thing all the time'. The implication is that such a practice is not only common but represents an improvement over the original composition, because words are added to it, making it into song and thus into discourse with an audience. That is, the 'ode' is made more like the type of music employed in MGM musicals. Peggy explains to Boroff that the score resulting from the 'tunes' the lyric writer dug up from the 'ode' will be 'commercial but with class'. This becomes the ideal blend for musical entertainment, stating precisely what popular and elite music have to offer each other. It is also a perfect description of the Freed Unit musical film (e.g. the **American in Paris** ballet). When we are finally shown a number from the film being shot to a playback, the song, *Josephine*, is an extremely jazzed-up version of Boroff, a parody of a typical MGM musical arrangement. Moreover, upon returning to Moscow, Boroff himself becomes fascinated with popular music, and we are shown his 'latest and most decadent composition', the jazz ballet *Red Blues,* a parody of an MGM 'high energy' production number with its 'folk' accompaniment (trumpet, accordian) and communal participation. At the end of *Red Blues,* Russian folk dances are incorporated into a frantic, upbeat, jazz choreography and musical arrangement, making the number yet another example of jazz overtaking and improving upon traditional music and dance. The Hollywood musical is uniquely equipped to blow its own horn. A film like **Silk Stockings** makes sure we recognize that horn as a jazz instrument.

The Red Blues in
Silk Stockings

4:

Dream Worlds and Dream Stages

**I'm afraid we're not in Kansas anymore.
We must be over the rainbow.**

Judy Garland, **The Wizard of Oz**

In one of the present-day sequences of **That's Entertainment, Part II,** Gene Kelly performs the trick of progressively eliminating colors from the abstract set on which he is singing:

What's left? Black and white,
But that's quite all right, it's entertainment,

to the familiar tune of *That's Entertainment.* The sequence provides a lead-in to clips from black and white films from the good old days of Hollywood. But the scene also produces an ironic twist on the way color was introduced into Hollywood musicals (and the way musicals were used to introduce color to the Hollywood audience). Studios progressively added color to provide more entertainment, that is, to increase the voluptuousness of those parts of a film which were supposed to represent fantasy. The first widespread use of technicolor occurred in 1929 when four musicals were shot entirely in technicolor, with over a dozen more containing color sequences in the form of musical numbers. Color made the numbers even more spectacular, increasing the contrast between musical number and spoken scene. Later, one of the first experiments in three-strip technicolor heightened the contrast between the dream of Oz and the reality of Kansas.

Even when all musicals came to be shot in color, some segments would be designated as more unreal than others by a more exaggerated use of color. **An American in Paris** introduces Leslie Caron through the other side of the looking-glass, as Georges Guetary describes for Oscar Levant his girl's infinite variety. We view Caron in a series of dance vignettes on mono-chromatic sets, the only color contrast provided by her costumes. Just prior to the colorful

American in Paris ballet, Minnelli gives us the Art Student's Ball entirely in shades of black and white so that, as he put it, 'when the black and white turned into color it would be so much more dramatic'. The ballet itself commences with the addition of color to a blow-up of a black and white charcoal sketch. The sketch represents Kelly's bleak vision of the loss of Leslie Caron; the ballet, in the vibrant colors of the French Impressionist palette, acts out that loss in symbolic form. Kelly's 1976 **That's Entertainment** appearance merely inverts the color values of his 1951 ballet by giving us a black and white fantasy world. Both films acknowledge levels of fantasy within musicals. Each film places a secondary, more stylized fictional world into a primary, less stylized fiction. The secondary, the unreal, the dream world holds at bay the imaginative excess to which musicals are prone. In the musical, as in life, there are only two places where we feel secure enough to see so vividly: in the theater and in dreams. The musical's multiple levels of reality contrast the stage with the world, illusion with reality.

Film theorist Peter Wollen has used the term 'multiple diegesis', meaning multiple narrative worlds, to refer to the heterogeneous narrative levels in post-1968 Godard films. In **Weekend**, *characters from different epochs and from fiction are interpolated into the main narrative... instead of a single narrative world, there is an interlocking and interweaving plurality of worlds.* ★

★ Peter Wollen, 'Counter Cinema: *Vent d'est'*, **Afterimage** (Autumn 1972) p.11

Multiple diegesis, according to this view, takes its meaning in antithesis to the 'single diegesis' of the classical narrative cinema. Both the Hollywood musical and modernist cinema use dual worlds to mirror within the film the relationship of the spectator *to* the film. Multiple diegesis in this sense parallels the use of the internal audience. Yet, as with the use of the distancing techniques described in an earlier chapter, the musical and Godard are worlds apart in their goals. In a Godard film, multiple diegesis may call attention to the discrepancy between fiction and reality, or fiction and history. In the Hollywood musical, heterogeneous levels are created so that they may be homogenized in the end through the union of the romantic couple. In the Hollywood musical, different levels are recognized in order that difference may be overcome, dual levels synthesized back into one.

Musicals are built upon a foundation of dual registers with the contrast between narrative and number defining musical comedy as a form. The dichotomous manner in which the story is told — now spoken, now sung — is a very different mode of presentation from the single thread of the usual Hollywood movie. The narrative with its third-person mode seems to represent a primary level. But unlike other kinds of movies, a secondary level, presented in direct address and made up of singing and dancing, emerges from the primary level. The first-person interruption disturbs the equilibrium of the unitary flow of the narrative but, as we have seen, in an entirely conventionalized manner. Proof that the break into song does indeed exist at a different level of reality may be seen in the way present-day audiences (if out of tune with the conventions) may greet with nervous laughter any transition between modes in the classic musical films.

In the backstage musical dual levels are apparent in the contrast between the backstage plot and the show or film within the film, between the world onstage and world offstage. Busby Berkeley musicals rope off the show as a separate universe, a world of cinematic excess and voyeuristic pleasure in sharp contrast to the low-budget verisimilitude of the backstage sequences. All of Berkeley's extravagant imagination gets bottled up within the show (he didn't even direct any of the narrative scenes prior to 1935). In the quasi-theatrical (but really cinematic) space of the Berkeley show transpires an absolutely unfettered play of the imagination. The Berkeley number epitomizes the show as secondary diegesis.

MGM Freed Unit musicals — in particular the films of Vincente Minnelli — often followed the backstage pattern of containing extremes of stylization in shows, but they also institutionalized a related practice — containing surrealistic decor and other excesses of style in dream sequences. Even within the bizarre universe of **Yolanda and the Thief** with its crimson-robed convent girls and painted mansions, explicitly Daliesque decor is reserved for the dream sequence. Dreams, as do shows, provide a secondary realm (the dream) more fantastic that a primary one (waking life). Dreams may

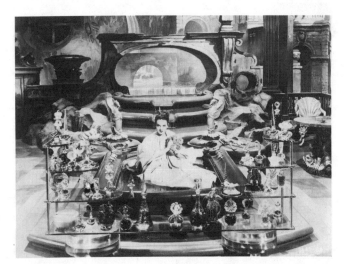

Reality in **Yolanda and the Thief**

render ordinary events surrealistic, making them a logical choice of instrument upon which to play the secondary register in the musical film.

The gap between the dream world and the practical world may be wide as in **The Wizard of Oz** or **Brigadoon**. In the latter film the distance between worlds is enormous, from midtown Manhattan to a Scottish fantasy kingdom. The gap is temporal as well, for Brigadoon comes to life only one day out of every century. Or the difference may be slim either because the 'real' world is already fantastic (**Love Me Tonight, The Pirate, Yolanda and the Thief**) or because the dreamer partakes of the mundane (as in **Bells Are Ringing**, where Judy Holliday spins her fantasies out of ordinary material). Yet there is always traffic between dream and reality. Unlike the Berkeley number, the dream world is never presented as an interchangeable part designed to fit almost any musical. It is always determined by the primary narrative realm. In **The Wizard of Oz**, as in **Cabin in the Sky, Lady in the Dark, Yolanda and the Thief**, and the influential stage production of **Oklahoma!**, the dream world is presented as the vision of one of the characters in the frame story. In **Cabin in the Sky**, dream angels and devils actually penetrate the primary world, whereas in **Oz**, the farmhands and Dorothy's fantasy companions are merely played by the same actors. Always the consciousness of the dreamer spans the worlds. In a striking scene in **Brigadoon**, Gene Kelly, back to the brittle reality of a Manhattan bar, hears (in the form of aural fantasies) little reprises of songs from the realm of Brigadoon, drowning out his fiancée's mundane conversation. Another Minnelli film, **On a Clear Day You Can See Forever**, locates the dream world within the

Gene Kelly hears music from Brigadoon in a Manhattan bar

70

unconscious of a remarkably ordinary girl. Inside Daisy lives Melinda, an English temptress of centuries gone by who comes to life only when Daisy is placed under hypnosis.

Given the models of the Berkeley spectacle and the Minnelli-Freed Unit dream sequence, one can speak of two forms which multiple diegesis takes in the musical. Some musicals carefully delineate dream and reality, narrative and spectacle, whereas others attempt to blend dream and reality, show and story. Yet this is ultimately a false dichotomy, a scholar's convenience, as is the distinction between the show and the dream. For in the musical, the show is the dream and the dream is the show. The Hollywood musical offers itself as the spectator's dream, the spectator's show. Any initial opposition between show and narrative, primary and secondary, dream and reality, is always collapsed by the musical's own narrative logic. Gene Kelly gets to return to Brigadoon which springs back to life out of the force of Kelly's desire. Dorothy returns to a Kansas transformed by her knowledge, however imaginary, of Oz.

Heterogeneous Worlds

In virtually every backstage musical from **42nd Street** in 1933 to **The Band Wagon** in 1953, the synthesis of the two levels depends on the marriage of the couple in the realm of the narrative occurring simultaneously with the success of the show in which they star. At a broader level the narrative resolution of every musical involves bringing together the forces of entertainment with forces opposed to entertainment. ★ The synthesis achieved through the union of the romantic couple always involves a reconciliation of values associated on the one hand with rational cognitive thought or even Puritanism (the reality principle) and on the other hand, the world of the imagination, the world of freedom, impulse, spontaneity, values which underlie the pleasure principle and entertainment. Usually, one member of the couple will represent reality, the other dreams (or one work, the other entertainment). Every marriage at the close of every musical also represents a merger of values. Very frequently at the end of a musical, only entertainment remains, reality having been obliterated by the force of the film itself.

In **Love Me Tonight**, two worlds are initially created in order to stress the synthesizing power of song. Unlike Kansas and Oz, the two realms — Maurice Chevalier's Paris and Jeanette MacDonald's mythical chateau — appear to be equally unreal. In both, people speak in rhymed dialogue, for example, whereas in **The Wizard of Oz** rhymed dialogue is spoken only in Munchkinland. *Isn't It Romantic?*

★ See Charles F. Altman, 'Toward a Theory of Genre Film', in **The 1977 Purdue Film Studies Annual, Part Two, Film: Historical-Theoretical Speculations,** (Pleasantville, New York: Redgrave, 1977) pp.31-43; and 'The American Film Musical: Paradigmatic Structure and Mediatory Function', **Wide Angle**, vol. 2, no.2 (January 1978) pp. 10-17.

connects the lovers in their separate worlds. Chevalier brings his kind of music from the entertainment kingdom of Paris to the sadly repressed kingdom over which MacDonald reigns, a world populated by old men moving in slow motion at twilight. After a dose of Chevalier's musical charm, the formerly stodgy inhabitants of the chateau wake up singing Maurice's naughty ditty, *Mimi*. In musicals as disparate as **Love Me Tonight, The Belle of New York, The Music Man, The Sound of Music** and **Silk Stockings**, a world of music transforms a repressed world of silence. Chevalier and Astaire just can't help singing and dancing over the objections of old men who can't make music themselves. In its most literal form, the process of bringing music to a world lacking in music is common to dozens of musicals. Metaphorically, all musicals provide such a synthesis for their audience by bringing music into their lives and, with luck, into their hearts. **Love Me Tonight** renders in exaggerated form this master synthesis of the genre.

In musicals which employ neither show nor dream, another strategy — the neutral meeting place — may substitute. Especially in 'folk' musicals, in which shows and dreams might appear too fanciful, there will often be a stylized set which stands apart from the dual spheres of the rest of the film and which ultimately mediates between them. In **The Harvey Girls**, the valley is the place where the couple may come together precisely because it is the place which can accommodate dreams emanating from the Alhambra Saloon as well as from the Harvey House Restaurant. The valley synthesizes civilization and savagery, amateur and professional entertainment, refinement and coarseness. In a rather poignant scene in the valley, Judy Garland tells

The valley in **The Harvey Girls**

John Hodiak that the couple can compromise 'no place in this world', implying that the valley, the place where the couple *can* compromise, is somehow 'out of this world'. The valley, a realm of fantasy, is that place where the narrative dualities of the film may be worked out in symbolic form prior to the plot's resolution. The valley shares with shows and dream sequences the idea of solving problems in one realm by virtue of an escape into the other.

Dream Sequences

To hear them described, there is a striking similarity between the function of multiple diegesis in musicals and the 'dream work' in Freudian dream interpretation. According to Freud, dreaming is a work, that is, a psychic process. At one point he describes the dream work as a secondary process. The primary process produces perfectly intelligible dream-thoughts; then in the secondary process these are worked into an irrational, oft-times 'surrealistic' form. Many dream sequences appear to be modeled on the Freudian dream work, with the dream diegesis as the irrational, stylized product of the secondary process. A handful of musicals acknowledge this structural debt to the father of psychoanalysis. **Carefree, Lady in the Dark** and **On A Clear Day You Can See Forever** take their plots from the psychoanalytic scenario with the dream world representing the unconscious of the dreamer. As the psychoanalyst portrayed by Fred Astaire explains it to Ginger Rogers in **Carefree**, there are two levels to the mind, the sub-conscious mind which dreams and the conscious mind which does not dream but rather thinks. The object of psychoanalysis, Fred Astaire style, is to bring the two into coordination. The more sophisticated among us might find this a ludicrous reduction of Freudian theory. They may neglect to notice, however, that it is a pretty good explanation of the synthesis between levels in musicals.

Unlike Freud, musicals suggest that this dream work acts as a kind of exorcism, leading to the actual fulfillment of desires. In dream sequences the parallel between the dream in the film and the dream that is the film is rendered most explicit. The Hollywood musical creates dream sequences within musicals in order to obliterate the differences between dreams in films, dreams in ordinary life, and dreams as the fulfillment in ordinary life of the promises offered by the movies.

Although not every dream sequence uses ballet in the strict choreographic sense, it's natural to refer to such interludes as dream ballets, since most of them do employ a narrative style of dance. The dream ballet as a set piece of the MGM musical of the 1940s and 1950s

73

had its roots in Broadway musical comedy. In 1937 George Balanchine started a craze by choreographing a dream ballet for **Babes in Arms**. Agnes de Mille's choreography for Laurey's dream in **Oklahoma!** in 1943 was followed by Robert Alton's choreography for Astaire in the **Ziegfeld Follies** (1944) and Eugene Loring's in **Yolanda and the Thief** (1945). *Limehouse Blues,* the Chinese fantasy sequence in **Ziegfeld Follies,** became a 'trial run' for the use of a more lengthy and balletic form of dance within a fantasy sequence. In the dream Astaire changed from his usual dance style (a combination of ballroom, tap, and a little ballet) to a more balletic one. Just as the colors of the dream world had to be more intense so its dance style had to be more stylized.

Dream ballets in MGM musicals emphasize either the wish of the dreamer (the *Pirate* ballet, the first dream ballet in **Lili**) or they represent a tentative working out of the problems of the primary narrative (**Yolanda and the Thief,** *A Day in New York* in **On the Town,** the *American in Paris* ballet, the second dream in **Lili**). ★ In those ballets which represent the dreamer's wish, the ballet foreshadows in symbolic form the eventual outcome of the plot. Those ballets which recapitulate the plot retrace the narrative in symbolic form to its point of rupture. The resolution of the narrative comes on the heels of the ballet, implying the dream ballet has been catalytic in resolving the film's narrative. Dream ballets of the problem-solving variety occur at a point when the initial dream of the principal dancer has fallen apart; it is up to the dream to put things back together again.

The wish ballet is more likely to occur early in the film as

★ *The Broadway Ballet* in **Singin' in the Rain** and *The Girl Hunt* in **The Band Wagon** bear a slightly more complicated relationship to their respective films since they are located in, respectively, a film and a show.

Laurey with her dream double in the film **Oklahoma!**

does a precursor of the MGM dream ballet, Ginger Rogers' dream dance with Astaire in **Carefree**. Ginger dreams she is dancing with her therapist (Astaire) a slow motion pas de deux to *I Used to Be Color Blind*. The dance meets all of the requirements for dream diegesis; as the lyric indicates, it was originally intended to be filmed in color; and the choreography in dreamy slow motion is full of balletic lifts found nowhere else in the series. And of course Ginger wakes up in love with Fred. Very often the wish ballet will allow the dreamer to road test various possible mates. Rogers' dreams in **Lady in the Dark** follow this pattern, as does Laurey's dream in **Oklahoma!**

The dream is the catalyst to falling in love in the real world. **The Pirate** establishes its orgiastic fire dance as a fantasy, and quite a sexual one, on the part of the repressed Manuela. Serafin the actor is transformed into Macoco, the Pirate, the man of Manuela's day dreams, now given a violently sexual charge. Similarly, the first dream ballet in **Lili** shows the child-woman played by Leslie Caron imagining herself in the glamorous garb of Zsa Zsa Gabor. The implication is that falling in love in dreamland is somehow transferable to the waking realm of the narrative.

The wish ballet establishes early in the film a problem-solving model which becomes explicit in the problem-solving type of dream ballet. Problem-solving dream dances tend to occur just prior to the denouement of the film, ending abruptly at that point where the primary story takes over and completes the ballet. The *American in Paris* ballet recapitulates the plot of the film as Kelly finds and loses the girl; at the ballet's conclusion the separation is rapidly resolved. At first glance, it seems odd to refer to this ballet as having a 'problem-solving' function, since the ballet begins and ends with Kelly holding a red rose instead of Leslie Caron. Similarly, at the end of *A Day in New York,* Kelly is still without Miss Turnstiles. And at the end of the dream in **Yolanda and the Thief**, Astaire wakes up in a cold sweat trapped in his bedsheets, suffering the same fear of entrapment presumably worked out in the dream sequence. The *American in Paris* ballet, like its predecessors in **Yolanda and the Thief** and **On the Town**, seems to have no narrative function at all in the sense of furthering the plot. All three sequences merely recap the primary story up to that point of rupture which initially precipitated the dream. The resolution always takes place in the primary diegesis, the 'real' world.

The second dream sequence in **Lili** illuminates the nature of problem-solving in the others as well. In the film Lili has fled from the lame puppeteer who loves her but who is unable to express his love except through the medium of the puppets. Lili, running away, skips down a road reminiscent of a set from Kansas in **The Wizard of Oz**. She imagines herself dancing with life-size figures of each of her

The second dream
sequence in **Lili**

beloved puppets. But each time, the puppet turns into the puppeteer
(Mel Ferrer) and Lili finds herself dancing with Ferrer, his powers
restored through her imagination. Through the agency of the dream-
fantasy, Lili realizes that Ferrer *is* the puppets and she rushes back into
the arms of the real puppeteer as the puppets, seemingly now detached
from their master, applaud the resolution of the film.

In a psychoanalytic model, the dream work consists in a
symbolization of repressed material, but the dream ballet permits a
kind of psychic cleansing process for the dreamer in the film which is
immediately transferable to the narrative. An analogy is created
among the primary diegesis of the musical, waking life in psychoanalysis, and the life of the spectator when the lights come up after the
film. Similarly, an analogy is created between the dream ballet, actual
dreams, and the experience of the film itself. The spectator 'wakes up'
after each. The dream ballet within the film represents the relationship
of the spectator *to* the film.

The experience of the film may provide an emotional
catharsis or an escape for the viewer, as the dream does for the dreamer
within the film. But when the musical also implies that dream ballets
resolve the very real problems of the narrative, and by analogy, that
movies fulfil our wishes in 'real life', the parallel between movies and
life breaks down. MGM musicals of the 1940s and 1950s don't dare to
question their own logic. To do so would be to deny the promise of
entertainment itself. For genre films serve the culture by working
through (in symbolic form) conflicts that can never really be resolved
outside the cinema. Out of this bottleneck emerge more and more
dream sequences, more and more Hollywood musicals.

The World and the Stage

The ultimate synthesis of the musical consists in unifying what initially was imaginary with what initially was real. These terms are always relative to each other within a given musical. But in the film's unfolding, the boundary between real and imaginary may be blurred. Musicals may project the dream into the narrative, implying a similar relationship between film and viewer. The dream resolution, the resolution of the film, and leaving the theater tend to occur within a very short time span. For a little while after seeing a musical, the world outside may appear more vivid; one may experience a sudden urge to dance down the street. The feeling of not knowing quite which world one is in may be evoked within the film as well. When a dream sequence is placed in the film *en abîme,* the fault line which separates illusion from reality is inevitably called into question. Peter Wollen says that,

> *in Hollywood films, everything shown belongs to the same world and complex articulations within that world — such as flashbacks — are carefully signaled and located.* ★

★ Peter Wollen,
'Counter Cinema:
Vent d'est', p.11

The transition to the dream in **Yolanda and the Thief** is an obvious exception to this rule. Fred Astaire, a jewel thief, has just denied he is thinking of Yolanda, the naive young heiress to the fortune of a mythical kingdom, whom he is attempting to rob. The camera cranes up from Astaire in bed and cranes over to a red carnation, as in **An American in Paris** a symbol of the woman. Presently Astaire, carnation in his lapel, dresses and goes out onto the street to a town plaza we have viewed in a previous scene in daylight — at that time a bystander had asked Astaire for a cigarette. Astaire's sojourn is accompanied by the song *Yolanda.* In a scene meant to evoke a feeling of déjà vu in the spectator, he follows the identical path we saw him take previously. This time, however, bizarre multiple arms emerge from the cigarette man. Eerie music comes up on the sound-track and the spectator, disorientated, begins to realize the film has entered a different diegesis from the previous visit to the town plaza. Soon showers of money start to fall on Astaire and he runs onto a surrealistic set with a gold and brown pavement (reminiscent of Yolanda's fortune and of Oz's yellow-brick road), statues of madonnas (reminiscent of Yolanda's garden) and live flamingos on a fake set (reminiscent of the title sequence). Heavily syncopated music overlaid with the jingle of coins comes up and Astaire starts moving to the beat and into a dance with a group of women in red (reminiscent of the girls at Yolanda's convent school). It is not until this point that the dance part of the dream begins. After the segment just described, the

77

The dream ballet in **Yolanda and the Thief** moves from the dream world of the plaza ...

to a Daliesque dance fantasy

camera cranes over to an even more explicitly surrealistic set — this one modeled on Dali. We have moved from the plaza set (recognizably part of the 'real' world of the fictional kingdom in which the film takes place) to the river set (clearly no longer belonging to a familiar world yet not clearly delineated as dream) to the wholly abstract Dali set (clearly a fantasy locale) for the major part of the dream sequence in which Astaire dances out his fears of entrapment.

The novelty of this sequence consists not so much in establishing parallels between dream and reality (all dream sequences do this) but rather in the impossibility of determining exactly where one leaves off and the other begins. The transition to the dream in **Yolanda** is one instance of a play on the boundaries between fantasy and 'reality' which informs the entire film. It is through cinematic technique that the boundaries between worlds are able to be blurred, placed *en abîme*. However, it is within the context of the show or film within the film that the connection between dream worlds and entertainment may be made.

A transition to a film-within-a-film, similar to the dream in **Yolanda**, occurs in **A Star is Born** (1954) in connection with *Born in a Trunk*. From a shot of Vicki Lester and Norman Maine (Judy Garland and James Mason) sitting in the audience at the premiere of Vicki's first musical film, with the sound of Vicki's voice off singing *Swanee,* there is a cut to Vicki doing a production number of *Swanee*. At first the spectator is given the film-within-the-film with masked-off black boundaries, calling attention to its internal status. Then from a cut to an angle backstage, the curtain is pulled shut and Vicki smiles at the chorus members. An audience applauds and there is a cut to an extreme long shot over the theater audience to Vicki in her minstrel costume taking a bow. We are shown shot-reverse shots from the film-within-the-film, plus inserts of Vicki and Norman watching the film (with the applause for Vicki within the film carrying over the cut). There is then a reverse shot of the film-within-the-film with masked borders filling our frame entirely as the *Born in a Trunk* monologue begins. The effect of this (actually quite brief) transition is difficult to describe but the disorientation seems to stem from confusion as to which audience is applauding for which show. The fact that this film-within-the-film is a backstage musical further confuses the distinction between movie theater, stage, and screen. The transition to *Born in a Trunk* places within the context of the film-within-the-film a questioning of the boundary between dream and reality, onstage and offstage, in order to emphasize the 'reality' of cinematic illusion and the 'fantasy' of actual experience (and vice versa).

Which is the dream world and which is the real world? If we can't tell the difference between illusion and reality, the musical film itself may appear just as 'real' as ordinary life. This illusion of reality that the merger of worlds gives to musicals works for both highly fantastical films and for *realistic* musicals. It seems obvious that **The Wizard of Oz** or **Yolanda and the Thief** legitimate a world of fantasy. But what of those musicals in which singing and dancing appear to emerge out of a perfectly normal narrative universe? Films such as **Meet Me in St Louis, On the Town** and **Bells are Ringing**, like those which are entirely fantastic, appear to have only one diegesis — the level of 'reality'. Yet within that single level, these films follow the same route as those more clearly dualistic. **On the Town,** famous for its location shooting and ordinary folk spirit, nevertheless interrupts its narrative just at the place where the hero's dream of finding the right girl in the dream world of New York has fallen apart. The dream ballet, substituting professional dancers for Kelly's non-dancing chums, adds to the film a dream register. Even when there is no dream dancing at all, musicals will follow the pattern of differentiating and then synthesizing a dream level and a reality level. The dream of **Meet Me in St Louis** is of the perfect family in the perfect rural setting, and of the technological paradise represented by the fair. That dream falls apart when the father tries to achieve progress at the cost of family unity. The moment of rupture when the world of the dreamer disintegrates takes the violent form of Tootie's destruction of the snow-family figures and of Esther's song:

> *Someday soon we all may be together*
> *If the fates allow*
> *Until then we'll have to muddle through somehow*

But the split between the dream of St Louis and the reality of New York is resolved when the father realizes that he can achieve both progress and family unity by staying right there in St Louis, the site of the fair itself, symbol of America's technological future. So too in **Bells are Ringing** does a dream world exist in the mind of a naturalistic character. Judy Holliday's dream is helping her clients at a telephone-answering service, by impersonating various fantasy characters on the phone, a dream that is realized when she falls in love with writer-client Dean Martin. Once again a poignant song *The Party's Over* calls attention to the loss of the dream. Yet in the end the dream is realized in the real world when all her clients come together to put on a show. In films which appear to have only one level — reality — the dreamer often tries to realize her fantasy in the real world. The numbers in such films seem part of the real world, so that when the dream is finally realized and both worlds are united, we feel the thrill of the possibilities for Utopian solutions to the problems of ordinary life.

The backstage musical links the fulfilment of a dream to the experience of entertainment. The eventually triumphant show brings together the life off the stage (the comic part of musical comedy) with and through the life on the stage (the musical part of musical comedy). In a typical backstage musical, the success of the couple will be placed in a metaphorical relationship to the success of the show. Often the characters make statements about the dream of love and the dream of the show that explicitly tie the two together.

In **For Me and My Gal,** Judy Garland and Gene Kelly make plans to get married immediately after playing their first matinée at the Palace Theater, the symbol of their theatrical dream in the film. In a typical pep-talk given by Fred Astaire to Judy Garland in **Easter Parade** after Astaire has refused to share billing with his former partner, Astaire analogizes between different kinds of dreams. He says that whereas some couples dream of settling down on a little farm, *their* dream is a 'spot' on a marquee. At the end of **The Band Wagon**, Cyd Charisse creates a metaphor between the 'long run' of the successful show and her anticipated long-lasting relationship with Astaire.

Frequently the couple plot and the show plot will intertwine onstage; very often the last shot of a backstage musical will be of the couple embracing onstage at the end of the successful show. In **Hello, Frisco, Hello**, an Alice Faye vehicle, the lovers are reunited by being brought onstage together to reprise the title song which they introduced long ago. In shows with motivated numbers the couple plot may be mirrored within the show as in **Kiss Me Kate** and **Cabaret**. Usually so sophisticated an interweaving occurs in more recent films, but one of the cleverest of such scenes occurred in the 1930 musical **Monte Carlo**. Jack Buchanan is masquerading as a hairdresser to gain the favor of Jeanette MacDonald. At the end of the film, everybody winds up at a comic opera whose plot concerns a hairdresser trying to win the favor of a lady! Scenes from the opera are intercut with plot scenes. Says the stuffy count to Jeanette in their box, 'It's a silly story only possible with music', implying that happy endings are only possible onstage. Jeanette replies, 'It's possible *without* music', implying a happy ending for herself and Buchanan in the 'real' world. Only in the musical can Jeanette seem more accurate than the count.

The musical's drive toward synthesis between fantasy and reality operates not only to create parallels between onstage and off, but also at times to prove that on and off are one and the same. **It's Always Fair Weather** ends up in a TV studio where the three ex-Army buddies find themselves on a 'This is Your Life'-type, live TV broadcast. The film's plot quite literally becomes the show, picked up by the live video cameras. Midway through **Holiday Inn**, in which Bing Crosby runs a resort hotel open only on holidays, a Hollywood company decides to make a film based on the Holiday Inn. We are shown a repeat of the *White Christmas* number now performed on an exact replica of the Inn built as a set in a Hollywood studio. And in films such as **Dancing Lady** and **Anything Goes**, the internal shows are described in such a way as to bear a suspicious resemblance to the film we have just been watching. 'All the world's a stage', said Shakespeare. 'The world is a stage, the stage is a world of entertainment', paraphrased Howard Dietz, lyricist of *That's Entertainment,* who was also head of publicity for MGM studios.

Traditionally a comic plot ends with a wedding, always a

symbolic festival celebrating the closure of the narrative, the restoration of order to the world. In the backstage musical the traditional wedding finale is connected with the life of the theater, stressing musical comedy's power to blend art and life. The ritual of closure is frequently celebrated onstage, archetypally in **You'll Never Get Rich,** a 1941 Fred Astaire - Rita Hayworth film which takes the conventions literally. The show can go on only if Rita agrees to star in it. But thinking that Astaire has two-timed her, she is about to marry a man she doesn't love and go off to Panama. Astaire must trick her on to the stage for the show whose finale — *The Wedding Cake Walk* — we are shown. What Hayworth does not realize until it is too late is that the marriage ceremony within the show is being performed by an actual chaplain hired by Astaire. The couple is thus married in both worlds during the finale of the show, surrounded by chorus girls all in bridal white. Although I can think of no other instance where the fate of couple and show are married quite so closely, the meaning of the wedding finale permeates the musical.

The standard Hollywood plot, as does the standard comic plot, ends with the union of the couple, all obstacles having been overcome. Many musicals elaborate on the final shot of the embracing couple by dissolving to a matched shot of the same couple in wedding dress. This wedding coda which follows the plot resolution exists outside the time and space of the film proper, becoming a celebration of the end of the film itself. The symbolic wedding celebrates the ongoing relationship between film and spectator as much as it celebrates the union of the couple (already well established by the first resolution). It's the difference between the finale of a Broadway

The Wedding Cake Walk — **You'll Never Get Rich**

82

The wedding coda to **Yolanda and the Thief**

musical and the bit of encore addressed to the audience at the curtain call.

Finale and coda to **The Pirate** must be viewed against this backdrop of musical-comedy convention. **The Pirate** substitutes (for the ritual dissolve to the couple in wedding garb) a dissolve to the couple in **clown** garb for the reflexive coda, *Be a Clown,* the ultimate celebration of illusionism. Now the resolution of the plot had demonstrated the triumph of the theatrical imagination released in Manuela by Serafin over the antiquated social system of the town. The 'fantasy' kingdom of the town in which Manuela dreams of the pirate Macoco becomes the 'reality' from which Manuela is liberated, first by journeying to the port city where she encounters Serafin; secondly by the unleashing of the performer within herself under hypnosis; finally, by the onstage revelation of the real Macoco in the form of the stodgy mayor (i.e. through theater). Forms of illusionism which can only lead to frustration — Manuela's unrequited longing for Macoco inspired by picture books and expressed in pirate-ballet fantasies — are replaced by theatrical illusionism. The theater too is a phantom form but one which is unifying, binding and achievable, and which liberates the dreamer from the constraints of day-dreaming. In short, the theatrical world stands for the cinema. In **The Pirate**, *Be a Clown* is the wedding coda addressed to the spectator. The end title to the film is

superimposed over the image of Serafin and Manuela (or is it Judy Garland and Gene Kelly?) dissolved in laughter. There is no implication that we need ever return to the drab reality Manuela faced at the beginning of the film.

Dorothy need never return to Kansas. Minnelli musicals closest to the center of the director's vision — **The Pirate** and **On a Clear Day You Can See Forever** — each end with the image of a projection of the actors into eternity, the former onstage and the latter into the dream world above the clouds. But the promise of eternal bliss 'over the rainbow' is not limited to Minnelli films. A Utopian, liberating vision lies at the heart of the musical genre. Even in **The Wizard of Oz**, Dorothy does not come back to the Kansas she left behind. Somehow the horror of that reality — embodied in the diabolical Miss Gulch — has been exorcized by the slaughter of the wicked witch in the dream world of Oz.

Musicals are unparalleled in presenting a vision of human liberation which is profoundly aesthetic. Part of the reason some of us love musicals so passionately is that they give us a glimpse of what it would be like to be free. We desperately need images of liberation in the popular arts. But the musical presents its vision of the unfettered human spirit in a way that forecloses a desire to translate that vision into reality. The Hollywood version of Utopia is entirely solipsistic. In its endless reflexivity the musical can offer only itself, only entertainment as its picture of Utopia. The very terms it set up for itself, however unconsciously, as an apology for mass art, prevented the musical from ever breaking out of its self-imposed hermetic universe.

The ritual marriage celebrated at the end of virtually every musical during the studio era was also a ritual celebration of a continuing marriage between Hollywood and the mass audience. During its years of popular favor the Hollywood musical externalized the dreams of countless filmgoers. Dream diegesis in the films was ultimately an attempt to validate this experience. In the 1950s as musicals fell out of favor, the films themselves started to question the easy equation between dreams, shows and falling in love. Perhaps the last step along the road away from the vision of the classical period is **All That Jazz** (1980) which terminates in the death of the artist and the negation of show business. Yet even in interrogating its own terms, the musical was bound by a form that had to remain essentially conservative.

A production
number from **All
That Jazz** combines
entertainment with
open-heart surgery

5:

The History of the Hollywood Musical:
Innovation as Conservation

The classical musical ends at that moment of perfect equilibrium when the couple is frozen into eternal embrace, the show frozen into a perpetually triumphant curtain call. It may seem as if this book has petrified the genre itself along the same lines. I have been speaking of 'the musical' as if it were a static structure, a hygienically sealed system free from the lint of changing audience tastes and of those historical transformations other forms seem to endure. But of course those of us who have watched **42nd Street** on the late show after an evening's cinema of **All That Jazz** know that musical comedy has altered from 1933 to 1980 with the culture surrounding it.

The classic period of the Freed Unit MGM musical may have extinguished its flame in the mid-1950s but musical entertainment endured and Hollywood musicals continued to be made. What seemed to die out in the mid-1950s was the energy at the heart of the great MGM musicals, an energy based on faith in the power of singing and dancing connected with an almost religious belief in Hollywood itself as the great inheritor of the spirit of musical entertainment. In 1944 it was perfectly possible to treat with high seriousness a scene in **Ziegfeld Follies** wherein The Great Ziegfeld 'passes the torch' to MGM's earthly representative, Fred Astaire. It was no accident that the golden age of the musical should terminate with the death of the old studio system that had spawned the genre. To be sure musicals continued to be made. Not all of them were as reflexive as **The Band Wagon**, itself a requiem for the studio musical. Nor were they all as critical of Hollywood as **A Star is Born** (1954). But if individual films remained within the classical canon, it remains true that the *genre* as an overriding structure which informs individual films (and yet which in a necessary paradox is also created from those films) underwent a transformation at the end of the studio era. This chapter will try to explain that transformation in the light of the idea that what we call the classical Hollywood musical is not a discrete entity, but rather one stage in a larger history of popular entertainment in the age of mass art.

Critics have noticed that film genres, especially long-lived ones such as the Western and the musical, follow a predictable life cycle. ★ After an early period in which the conventions themselves seem fresh and noteworthy, genres have to keep giving us something new without sacrificing the appeal those conventions held in the first place, an appeal based on cultural rituals celebrated in genre films and an appeal that made the genre popular to begin with. Film-makers, that is, need to acknowledge within genre films the audience's growing familiarity with the language of the genre, their increasing generic literacy. Late genre films tend to expose the structure itself at the expense of a transparent conduction of the ritual value the genre carries. Many have noted a movement in Westerns toward parody and even auto-critique in films such as **The Man Who Shot Liberty Valance, Cheyenne Autumn**, and **The Shootist**. The latter film even goes so far as to place within its narrative a flashback to scenes from the career of the legendary (and presumably fictional) gunfighter John Wayne portrays in the film, a sequence composed entirely of recognizable scenes from earlier John Wayne Westerns. The overall pattern seems to develop from an early un-selfconscious conveyance of cultural mythology to a twilight period of reflection and even self-criticism.

★ The best discussion of this phenomenon is in Thomas Schatz, **Hollywood Genres** (New York: Random House, 1981).

The Hollywood musical does not concern itself with the lives of Great American Heroes, but the later career of Fred Astaire (discussed below) follows a pattern identical to that of John Wayne, in which Astaire's own career and myth form the subject matter for his last dances. The backstage musical would seem to exemplify such an evolutionary description of a genre's development. Looking only at the transformations of the basic syntax — the equivalence of the success of the couple with the success of the show — it's possible to outline a periodization of the backstage sub-genre marked by key films which added something new to that syntax.

From the 1929 **Broadway Melody** there emerged a combination that with some modification would become the means of identifying the backstage species. Romantic performing couples intermingle with shows, but the successful equation of the two is missing, for Bessie Love as half of a sister act must sacrifice personal happiness for her success on the stage while her sister finds true love but must sacrifice a life in the theater. Although there exists a long-

88

standing melodramatic strain in the popular imagination associating the actor's life with personal suffering, that combination was hardly suited to the rhetoric of the Hollywood musical. It was a series of Warner Bros backstage musicals emerging in 1933 that established the backstage musical as musical *comedy*. From this point on, the libido that drives the young lovers would be equated with the energy that puts the show on the stage. **42nd Street** begins to put the combination together as Ruby Keeler goes out to become a star and obtains the young crooner Dick Powell as well. But as yet the force behind Ruby's participation in the show remains separate from the sexual force. Director of the show, Warner Baxter, remains on the periphery of the love plot. Very soon Warner Bros backstage musicals would correct this imbalance, allowing for the perfect doubling of the world off the stage and the world of the stage as dual comic universes. In **Footlight Parade** the director, Jimmy Cagney, participates in the *Shanghai Lil* number of the final triumphant prologues he as director has devised. In **Gold Diggers of 1933** and **Dames** it is the young Dick and Ruby figures whose enthusiasm for each other weds with their desire to put on a show. When Busby Berkeley, director of the musical sequences for these early backstage sagas, went to MGM in the 1940s, the resulting Mickey Rooney - Judy Garland films showed even more clearly that the backstage musical was the classic evocation of the parallel between love and work that only the theater could provide. At last the world had become a stage, the stage a world *of entertainment*. The triumph of couple and show that dominated the classical period was so much taken for granted that by the early 1950s, the most ordinary Hollywood musicals assumed the dualism automatically. **Somebody Loves Me**, an undistinguished 1952 biography of singer Blossom Seeley and her partner Bernie Fields, motivates nearly every onstage number according to the vicissitudes of the love plot.

Yet at the same time — during the late 1940s and early 1950s — a subtle change was taking place under the impetus of those backstage vehicles produced by MGM's Freed Unit and scripted by Betty Comden and Adolph Green. The equation between couple and show remained, but it seemed to be shouted perhaps too loudly with a stridency suggesting the faith needed to be reaffirmed. **The Barkleys of Broadway, Singin' in the Rain** and **The Band Wagon** all challenged the sacred duality of romantic love and a hit show only in order to see it make a comeback by the final credits. Then **A Star is Born** took the Comden and Green logic to an extreme, splitting the couple down the center in a significant way for the first time since 1929. ★ When Judy Garland announces her comeback as 'Mrs Norman Maine' the equation is reaffirmed but a tragic afterimage lingers on, especially since the death of Norman Maine was motivated by Hollywood itself.

★ An occasional film did this during the studio period, notably **Ziegfeld Girl** (1941), which, however, paralleled the tragic couple with two comic couples.

The past twenty five years have seen various experiments in twisting the old formulas with the clearest new combination — **All That Jazz** (1980) — culminating in the death of the director and an ironic use of Ethel Merman's anthem to damn entertainment rather than celebrate it. The formula of the classical period seems to have been perfectly inverted, now insisting that art is not life and indeed that the accomplishment of entertainment must inevitably be at the expense of one's personal happiness.

The backstage musical provides a textbook illustration of a genre's development from a period of experimentation in which the conventions are established (1929-33) to a classical period during which a balance reigns (1933-53) to a period of reflexivity dominated by parody, contestation and even deconstruction of a genre's native tongue. Indeed, the neat unfolding I have just been enumerating has about it an almost mathematical precision, as if one could out of a table of permutations have predicted the emergence of certain new combinations at certain periods in the genre's history.

But a crucial factor is left out of an explanation of the musical's development as an ever-more-complex variation on a single theme. That forgotten truth is the backstage musical's congenital reflexivity. Early Westerns are about the coming of civilization and law to an untamed wilderness; late Westerns may question the value of civilization by reflecting ironically upon earlier examples of the genre. But early musicals are already about putting on shows. The musical's inherent reflexivity may lead to a different account of its development from that of other Hollywood genres which refer more directly to the world outside their boundaries. Early musicals have embedded within them earlier or different versions of the same text — in this case the reigning forms of popular theatrical musical entertainment at the time Hollywood musicals emerged. The Hollywood musical as a chapter in the history of popular theatrical entertainment could keep pace with a fickle mass audience by including within itself different generations or species of entertainment.

What makes the musical unique among film genres is not so much that its heyday neatly coincides with the studio years, but rather that its reflexive capability rendered it that genre whose explicit function was to glorify American entertainment while at the same time being itself a form of entertainment (as were all genre films). Other genres could become increasingly self-critical or socially critical as the audience outgrew the more simplistic statements of an earlier era without having to confront the dilemma of seeming to criticize mass entertainment itself. It was always easier for the Hollywood musical to see entertainment in a positive light. Even in the post-studio era, musical films which criticized the whole myth of musical entertainment had to proceed along essentially conservative lines so long as the films themselves purported to be examples of mass entertainment.

The Comden and Green films of the early 1950s found an ingenious solution to the problem of acknowledging the passage of time while at the same time glorifying entertainment tradition. Such an unveiling and re-veiling of entertainment's mystique operates across time as well. The Band Wagon demystifies earlier forms of live theater and stars of past eras. Singin' in the Rain demystifies silent movies, serious theater and early talkies while glorifying musical comedy. In both films, however, the parody of earlier entertainment forms is so affectionate that it might as well pass for praise. Indeed we have a common term to describe remystification in a sentimental vein. That term, nostalgia, is frequently used in reference to musical comedy. So many musicals try to evoke nostalgia for bygone entertainment eras, while at the same time asserting that entertainment itself is eternal. When, in the finale of The Band Wagon, the assembled cast and chorus sing,

> A show that is really a show
> Sends you out with a kind of a glow
> And you say as you go on your way
> That's entertainment

they are no longer referring to the internal show but to the film itself.

Although not every musical appears on the surface to be about the demystification of earlier forms of its own species, it is nevertheless possible to tell the history of the *genre* as the story of a continuing cycle of conservation within innovation, or, to put it in a more radical perspective, of innovation *as* conservation. If we view the Hollywood musical as one phase in the history of musical entertainment, we must refute the commonly held belief that the musical declined or died out in the 1950s. Instead we must see that the musical was transformed as the industry was transformed, with the positive reflexive function being transferred to the new mass medium, television. Meanwhile, the more critical function remained with the cinema in the less mass-orientated musical films which continued to be made (Cabaret, New York, New York, All that Jazz) and even more significantly, in the critical role taken up by more elitist types of cinema (Godard) and by film criticism itself.

Never in the Hollywood musical do we get an unqualified critique of mass entertainment itself. Even All That Jazz ultimately glorifies the director's art at the expense of his life, with his death portrayed as a razzle-dazzle production number in the best Bob Fosse style. An alumnus of MGM, Fosse can afford to be cynical about entertainment as long as he's still giving it to us in the process. Within

91

the mass-distribution system, the Hollywood musical doesn't dare to take entertainment values out of musical performance. To be sure, Hollywood frequently made bad musicals that weren't entertaining, but it never set out to do so as Godard does in his distinctly unmusical interludes with distinctly non-singing and non-dancing stars. When Gene Kelly dances in the street, we may be lulled into thinking we could do the same; when Anna Karina and Jean-Paul Belmondo dance in the street, we know we could do the same and we also know we wouldn't want to. To dare not to be entertaining is the ultimate transgression, the ultimate form of reflexivity as critique. For to be unentertaining means to think about the base upon which mass entertainment itself is constructed.

If in one sense the musical gets more and more self-reflexive at both positive and negative poles as it tries to outrun audience familiarity with its conventions, in another sense the musical does not change at all. The materials with which musical entertainment builds change across time, but the process of nostalgia for the old and mystification of the new never changes. Musicals are rerun, reissued, remade and revived. **The Wizard of Oz** is shown every year on American network television. The American Film Institute reissued the Astaire-Rogers series in new 35mm prints. **Meet Me in St Louis** encouraged numerous imitations which quoted from the original. Many films from the 1929-33 period were later remade. At the time of this writing, **The Jazz Singer** is being remade. Numbers from MGM musicals were clipped for **That's Entertainment,** just as Eleanor Powell's production number from **Born to Dance** had turned up intact in **I Dood It.** In each case older or different musicals are recycled

A reference to vaudeville in *Born in a Trunk* — **A Star is Born**

92

The medicine show in **High, Wide and Handsome**

into new ones. At the same time the musical seems to be saying 'we don't need that anymore', it also seems to be saying, 'because we *are* that ourselves'. As early as 1932, **Love Me Tonight** satirized a run of operettas that had preceded it, all the while being itself a MacDonald-Chevalier operetta.

The musical's dual structure lends itself to a process of growth through recycling that would be the envy of any environmentalist. Historically this process may be seen as the incorporation of earlier or different entertainment forms into current musicals. Backstage musicals quote liberally from theatrical sources; the *Born in a Trunk* sequence from **A Star is Born** represents a virtual compendium. Even the folk musical is full of longing for all varieties of archaic entertainment forms: the cakewalk in **Meet Me in St Louis**; saloon entertainment in **The Harvey Girls**; the medicine show in **High, Wide and Handsome**; the magic lantern show in **Centennial Summer**, to mention just a few. As a new generation of musical films developed out of the previous one, quotations tended to come from earlier musical films. **Singin' in the Rain**, for instance, is about early musical films, not vaudeville. **Cover Girl** in 1944 flashed back to vaudeville; **Xanadu** in 1980 places side by side the star of **Cover Girl** and Olivia Newton-John's disco rollerskating. Gene Kelly even has the same name ('Danny McGuire') in each film. A third source of material for new musicals might be called the 'extra-filmic' as it involves material connected to a performer's life and reputation outside the film. We shall examine the way in which Judy Garland's post-MGM films fed upon the public's knowledge of her unstable personal life.

From all this emerges a pattern of historical succession.

Earlier Hollywood musicals tend to quote from the previous generation of live entertainment, using these earlier forms for the shows within the films. Later Hollywood musicals quote from the same live forms but also begin to use material from earlier Hollywood musicals and from familiar star personas (I use the term 'persona' to refer to the star's image as created by his or her films). Post-studio musicals (television shows, compilation films and the 'nostalgia industry' included) in turn incorporate material from the 'golden age' of the studio-era musical, playing on our feelings for the performers of that era. In a sense the history of popular entertainment in America is rewritten as the show-within-a-film in musical entertainment. The materials change, but the process remains constant. The earlier form is recycled into the contemporary form, in the process cancelling through quotation any discontinuities between the audience and the entertainment industry. Instead of a process of creation and cancellation, what we actually have in a historical sense is a process of quotation and cancellation, for nothing wholly new is ever really 'created'. Across time the synthesis of past and present entertainment forms cancels the distinction between old and new forms of entertainment, so that musical shows appear simultaneously revolutionary and traditional. Entertainment comes to exist in a perpetual present which is also a perpetual past.

Non-Filmic Sources to Filmic Sources During the Studio Era

In the 1970s, films such as **That's Entertainment** and **New York, New York** looked nostalgically back at the Golden Age of the Hollywood musical. In much the same way, Hollywood musicals of the Golden Age had frequently borrowed from live-entertainment formats, sometimes from contemporary forms but often from the recent entertainment past. The two most common sources for the internal shows in backstage musicals were the theater and popular songs.

Theatrical Sources

Just as the folk musical looks back upon a Utopian version of the American past, backstage musicals hark back to more sentimental and communal forms of entertainment. Two of these theatrical forms, the revue and vaudeville, thrived on the New York stage prior to the emergence of the musical film in the mid-1920s. Neither revue nor vaudeville used narrative to bind together the numbers and to bind the spectator to the numbers. Both were variety formats based on a series of isolated acts. After the first few years of its existence, the Hollywood musical rarely used the revue format, preferring the more integrated musical-comedy structure. Yet within the films, vaudeville never died. The variety formats identified the inner show as earlier and less manipulative than contemporary forms. Such a choice implies a dualistic statement: the smart, sophisticated modern Hollywood musical nevertheless maintains the communal bonds of the earlier theatrical forms.

Even an 'integrated' theatrical form may symbolize an earlier era. As did vaudeville and revue, operetta represented a recently popular theatrical form eclipsed in popularity by musical comedy. Since many film musicals of the 1930s were adapted from stage operettas, the Hollywood musical was able to assimilate into its own structure the recent theatrical past. Minstrel shows and melodramas evoke an even earlier and folksier entertainment era than that of 1910-30. Both thrived in the nineteenth century, one or more generations removed from the musical film. And both take on nostalgia value when employed in the amateur entertainments of the Mickey Rooney - Judy Garland musicals or in the *Born in a Trunk* sequence of **A Star is Born**.

But of all the formats used in backstage musicals, the show boat is the one that takes the idea of folk relations most seriously, for what was a show boat but a proscenium stage that travelled down the river to greet its audience? Nowhere do we get a folksier, more informal and spontaneous internal show than in the 1936 film **Show**

The minstrel show
in **Babes in Arms**

Boat when Captain Andy interrupts the show to read messages to members of the audience. Hollywood seized upon this symbolic potential in filming **Show Boat** in 1929, 1936, and 1951 (not to mention the condensed version in **Till the Clouds Roll By**). Since all these theatrical sources quoted as inner shows in musicals evoke nostalgia for live entertainment, the very act of quotation means that the forms are not lost but rather reincarnated in the newer form, the musical itself.

Popular Song:
Musical Biopics and the Recycling of Songs

1911: In a fabulous and beloved era, near enough to be warmly remembered, two bright and shining stars, Vernon and Irene Castle, whirled across the horizon into the hearts of all who loved to dance. This is their story. ★

★ Printed title at the beginning of **The Story of Vernon and Irene Castle**

It would seem that at one time or another, every composer, bandleader and entertainer who ever graced the stage or screen has had his or her life immortalized in a Hollywood musical biopic. Each ensuing generation in this way paid tribute to the artists of the preceding generation of entertainment. The notion of a past 'near enough to be warmly remembered' is at the heart of this nostalgic impulse because it implies 'but long enough dead to be sentimentalized'.

Many of the entertainers and most of the song-writers portrayed in the biopics of the 1940s and 1950s provided music for Hollywood musicals as well. The biopic could use the writing of the numbers for its narrative with the performances of those same numbers as the spectacle, counting on the film audience's nostalgia for the popular songs of a bygone era. The narratives may identify musical-comedy material as 'the real American folk music', as in the Jerome Kern biography **Till the Clouds Roll By** in which Kern's 'little tunes' are identified as 'the real music, the folk music of America'. Then the film can move on to associate that material with the MGM musical itself. The Rodgers and Hart biopic, **Words and Music**, portrays the duo writing their legendary Broadway triumphs, then moving on to Hollywood where they encounter the 'real-life' Judy Garland at a party and she just happens to sing a few numbers.

Composers' biopics displayed the songs of American popular composers in their original showcases. Aside from the biopics, the cleverest way of mining the song catalogues of Gershwin and friends was a practice identified with Arthur Freed of building original musicals around these well-worn songs. Even when the

96

Ragtime Violin – part of the nostalgic Irving Berlin medley in **Easter Parade**

narratives are contemporary backstage stories, the songs carry the continuity from the previous generation. Many of the best-known film musicals were built on this sort of quotation: MGM's **An American in Paris** (Gershwin), **The Band Wagon** (Dietz and Schwartz), and **Singin' in the Rain** (Freed and Brown); and Paramount's **Holiday Inn** and **Blue Skies** (Irving Berlin). **Easter Parade** goes it one better, combining old standards of Irving Berlin with new songs written by the composer for that film, imbuing the new songs with the familiar quality of the old tunes. Moreover, the turning point in the film's narrative comes when Garland discovers her true performing identity as the offstage world dissolves into an onstage medley of Berlin perennials introduced by *I Love a Piano*. **Easter Parade** takes advantage of the length of Berlin's career to remind us that sheet music for the piano provided a means of distribution for hit songs in the days before mass media.

As the genre aged, old standards from Broadway and Tin Pan Alley combined with those written for earlier film musicals in keeping with an overall movement from non-filmic to filmic sources. Most of the songs in **Singin' in the Rain** (1952) were written for earlier Hollywood musicals. Nothing succeeds better at evoking nostalgia than the popular songs of an earlier era. By inserting old songs into new narratives, the Hollywood musical could have the best of both generations. Ironically, today most people cannot distinguish original film musical scores from recycled ones. For the audience of **That's Entertainment**, all quotations come from filmic sources.

Fred Astaire and Ginger Rogers
from Vernon and Irene Castle to Josh and Dinah Barkley

With the passage of time, an earlier generation of film musicals became nostalgia films upon which new musicals could draw. Some of the great musical stars had been with us for a long time. The audience remembered their old films and the aura surrounding those films. In 1939, audiences remembered the once-legendary dancing team Vernon and Irene Castle, commemorated on film by the then-legendary team of Fred Astaire and Ginger Rogers. By 1949, Astaire and Rogers themselves had passed into legend, and could summon in **The Barkleys of Broadway** memories of their own special Art Deco luster.

The Story of Vernon and Irene Castle was the last of the Astaire-Rogers RKO series that dominated the 1930s' musical. **The Barkleys of Broadway**, the product of another longstanding production unit under producer Arthur Freed at MGM, reunited Astaire and Rogers ten years after the RKO series ended. The two films provide a vivid example of the way in which the quoting films of one generation become the quoted films of the next, and of the way in which theatrical and filmic sources could work together in a complex blend of mystery and unveiling.

Arlene Croce has described how the RKO series fed upon its own filmic flesh to churn out Astaire-Rogers musicals for an insatiable public. ★ Each ensuing film would take its plot from the next-to-last film in the series. Films which came three-quarters of the way through the series, **Swing Time** (released September 1936) and **Shall We Dance** (released May 1937) already quote from preceding films of the series, in the process commenting on the mythical 'Fred and Ginger' those films had created. **Swing Time** works by inverting the glamorous aura of the earlier film, **Top Hat**. Already we see in miniature the process of quotation through which a genre grows.

Vernon and Irene seems to turn the series inside out in a far more drastic way than **Swing Time** inverted Astaire's **Top Hat**. Where the other films were light-hearted and high keyed in both spirit and lighting, **Vernon and Irene** seems entirely more somber, its atmosphere lighting and melodramatic plot incongruous for musical comedy but representatives of a melodramatic undercurrent that tended to surface in biopics. As Vernon and Irene, Astaire and Rogers appear to renounce the very star personas which had made the series a success. Astaire and Rogers no longer dance in their own special style. The hitherto contemporary settings are removed to a nostalgic past. The songs are the standard tunes of that pre-World War One era as opposed to the original contemporary scores of the series proper.

★ The following discussion is indebted to Arlene Croce, **The Fred Astaire and Ginger Rogers Book** (New York: Galahad Books, 1972).

Most shocking of all, the ineffable, immortal Fred Astaire dies at the end of the film.

It is as if **The Story of Vernon and Irene Castle** was made to commemorate the end of the series, the death of 'Fred and Ginger'. **Vernon and Irene** is at once the last film in the series (demystifying that series) and the first nostalgia film for Fred and Ginger. Far from being insensitive to the audience, the film takes the emotions of the mass audience into account, allowing the viewers to mourn the end of the series through a process of cancellation in the film itself. ★ In quoting the fictionalized lives of the historical entertainment figures, Vernon and Irene Castle, the film mystifies the RKO series. In evoking nostalgia for the 'real' figures of an earlier era, the film evokes as well nostalgia for the 'reel' figures of Fred and Ginger, figures too near and too warmly remembered to introduce directly.

The biopic works by setting up parallels between the story of Vernon and Irene Castle and the story of Fred Astaire and Ginger Rogers, affecting a transfer of nostalgia from one to the other. The film strongly implies that what Vernon and Irene represented to the pre-war generation, Astaire and Rogers represent to the present decade (the 1930s) — mass-culture figures. By setting up this parallel, the film is able to work on seemingly contradictory levels. It is able to defamiliarize Fred and Ginger, yet also evoke nostalgia for their embodiment in a decade of films. Take, for example, the scene of Vernon's and Irene's debut as professional ballroom dancers. Expecting to dance the following evening, the Castles instead are called upon to perform spontaneously. The spark of spontaneity contributes to their success as the dance spreads to other couples on the floor. The film then dissolves to the rise-to-fame montage sequence as the whole country dances in step with Vernon and Irene. Although the Castles' dance is not in the Astaire-Rogers style (which is both jazzier and more balletic), it nevertheless recalls similarly spontaneous dances in the series proper, the famous rehearsal dances, for instance. In this way quotations from earlier forms of live entertainment may evoke earlier films as well.

By the time MGM made **The Barkleys of Broadway**, the RKO series as a whole had become the near and warmly remembered entertainment past with Astaire and Rogers as the legendary figures of that era. Although in **The Barkleys** Astaire and Rogers play theatrical luminaries, the couple does not regress to a past era of entertainment. Theatrical precedents for **The Barkleys** would register as far less significant to the film's audience than its references to the careers of Fred Astaire and Ginger Rogers. During the late 1930s and 1940s Rogers' popularity had for a time eclipsed Astaire's. But when she attempted 'serious' roles, their fortunes reversed. **The Barkleys**

★ Such a use of discourse with the audience is a common phenomenon on television, another medium where a close and continuous association between stars and audience is built up over a period of years. During the 1976-7 American TV season, both **The Mary Tyler Moore Show** and the American broadcast of **Upstairs, Downstairs** had terminating episodes which were elegiac in nature.

99

Echoes of Fred and
Ginger in **The
Barkleys of
Broadway**: *Swing
Trot* ...

*... My One and
Only Highland
Fling*

celebrates the team's reunion, the fact that they are, as the advertising
put it, 'joyously together again'. Yet the film also makes Ginger
Rogers pay a ritual penance for having deserted Fred Astaire, musical
comedy, and the mass audience in the intervening years.

     Astaire's and Rogers' career chronicles (at least as the public
imagined them to be) unfold and are resolved in symbolic form within
the world of the Barkleys. Even though the film was initially written
for Astaire and Garland, its plot recapitulates both the romance of
'Fred and Ginger' and the problems Fred Astaire and Ginger Rogers
suffered as a result of their professional divorce. Not only must Ginger

endure a ritual spanking but the very terms of the earlier partnership must be questioned and then mystified anew. As did **Vernon and Irene, The Barkleys** works through problems at two levels, replaying the saga of the Astaire-Rogers parting all the while invoking the cinematic history of Fred and Ginger. From the opening number which runs under the titles (*Swing Trot*), one would never guess that Fred and Ginger had once tried to impersonate Vernon and Irene, so reminiscent is it of their old fast routines. Almost every number in **The Barkleys** quotes one of the old favorites. *My One and Only Highland Fling* harks back to the gimmick duets such as the dance on roller skates to *Let's Call the Whole Thing Off. Shoes With Wings On* evokes other Astaire trick solos, *Bojangles of Harlem* for instance. The rehearsal number in **The Barkleys** rings familiar as well in all its wondrous spontaneity. One number, however, doesn't just allude to a love song from Fred's and Ginger's youth but quotes it word for word. *You Can't Take That Away From Me,* sang Fred to Ginger in **Shall We Dance**. The Gershwin song was added to **The Barkleys'** Harry Warren-Ira Gershwin score when Rogers replaced Garland. In its original setting, the Gershwin tune commemorated Fred's and Ginger's brief marriage. **The Barkleys** gives the song more resonance than it ever could have had in the 1930s. In its new surroundings the song seems to refer to the memorable partnership of Astaire and Rogers. Not only was the repetition of the song nostalgic, but the content wanders down memory lane as well in its references to 'never, never meeting again' and 'always, always keeping the memory'. Compounding the richness of the quotation is the dance Astaire and Rogers add to the song for **The Barkleys**, redolent of their legendary romantic duets.

All these musical throwbacks to the 1930s rest within a suspiciously familiar plot. Josh and Dinah Barkley are a legendary musical comedy team who quarrel over Dinah's theatrical ambitions. Josh had 'made' Dinah as his dancing partner (a metaphor brought out in a scene where the Barkleys view a sculpture of themselves portrayed as her pancake to his frying pan). But now she appears to have declared her independence from musical comedy. The Barkleys begin *They Can't Take That Away From Me* out of public pressure, but they end it joyously together again. At the end of the film Josh and Dinah reunite in a lap dissolve from offstage to onstage resolving never again to forsake 'fun set to music'. Every movie-goer alive in 1949 would have recognized in the Barkleys the story of Fred Astaire and Ginger Rogers. And who among them would not rejoice at the resolution? No more Sarah Bernhardt for Ginger, no more mourning for the audience. At the same time that the backstage plot chastizes Ginger Rogers for deserting the musical-comedy audience that Astaire had created her for, the numbers are there to make us feel nostalgia for Fred and Ginger, implicitly forgiving Ginger now that she has come back to Fred at last.

Conservative Reflexivity

A combination of theatrical, filmic and extra-filmic quotation served as building blocks for musicals of the 1950s. Although the reflexivity inherent in such a process presents itself most clearly for view in self-conscious films like **The Barkleys** or **The Band Wagon**, almost every musical of the studio's twilight years had to rely on one or another brand of quotation from prior sources. Later, post-studio musicals would quote from the great films and great stars of the studio years. Just as **The Barkleys** could ignore the distinction between Vernon and Irene and the others, musicals of the 1970s (archetypally the compilation film **That's Entertainment**) could ignore the differences between early and late studio musicals. Filmic sources for musicals are easily summarized in table form (see Table 1).

The enduring musicals of the 1950s contain a large percentage among them of highly self-conscious films: the Comden and Green collaborations; other MGM musicals seemingly quite aware of their own status as entertainment products (**Lili, Silk Stockings, Les Girls**); Warners' **A Star is Born** and Paramount's **Funny Face**, both the work of MGM alumni such as Garland and Roger Edens. All films of the 1950s inevitably quote more for the simple reason that there were more films to quote from and fewer new twists to old formulas. If the self-conscious films quote with the purpose of remystifying, other films of the period seem to quote

Table 1: Filmic Quotation

Quoting film	Sources
Centennial Summer (1946)	
State Fair (1945)	
Summer Holiday (1946)	**Meet Me in St Louis** (1944)
On Moonlight Bay (1951)	
Has Anybody Seen My Gal? (1952)	
The Jolson Story 1947)	Jolson persona
Jolson Sings Again (1950)	**The Jolson Story**
Easter Parade (1948)	Astaire-Rogers; Garland's 'folk' persona
The Barkleys of Broadway (1949)	Astaire-Rogers; Rogers solo
Show Boat (1951)	**Show Boat** (other versions)
Royal Wedding (1951)	Astaire's stage career; Astaire's film persona
Belle of New York (1952)	The Astaire legend
Singin' in the Rain (1952)	Early Hollywood musicals
The Band Wagon (1953)	Astaire; economic condition of studio
A Star is Born (1954)	Judy Garland; the MGM musical
The Country Girl (1954)	Bing Crosby's 'cool' persona
It's Always Fair Weather (1955)	Kelly persona **On the Town** (television)
Silk Stockings (1956)	Astaire as 'Mr Entertainment'; Esther Williams
Funny Girl (1968)	Fanny Brice/Barbra Streisand
Funny Lady (1975)	legends
That's Entertainment (1974 and 1976)	The MGM musical/ **The Band Wagon**
All That Jazz (1980)	The ode to entertainment **A Star is Born** (1954)

merely because they have nothing new to say. Two Doris Day vehicles released by Warners in 1951 are almost total pastiches of older musicals. **Lullaby of Broadway** quotes from the famous Busby Berkeley number in the image of the far-away head of Doris Day singing against a black backdrop. **On Moonlight Bay** quotes from **Meet Me in St Louis** its image of a Victorian midwestern street emerging from a freeze frame. In both cases the quotation is visual and iconic, not merely narrative or musical.

Quotation in the late-studio and post-studio musicals didn't necessarily mean a deconstruction of the genre. Most of the time, it represented a mere borrowing from already existing sources. All forms of quotation which eventually reaffirm continuity with the past might be termed 'conservative' or 'constructive'. Almost every post-studio film which itself relies on entertainment values must in some way affirm the old. The many Broadway adaptations of the 1950s and 1960s certainly did this in the care they took to preserve the original form of the Broadway show. Nostalgia films such as **The Boy Friend** or **That's Entertainment** have conservation as their *raison d'être*. Although we don't think of **That's Entertainment** as a musical with narrative and numbers, it's possible to let history give it a double register. Unlike reissues and revivals which quote entire films verbatim, **That's Entertainment** quotes only the numbers from MGM musicals, replacing the original narratives with an explicitly nostalgic narration by the stars of days gone by. Just as Freed had built 'original' musicals around a composer's songs, it is now those very 'original' numbers which are being quoted, not merely the songs. The nostalgic narration, as ever, acts to bind the spectator to the heightened reality of the numbers. In **Part II**, source and quotation occupy the same frame as the 'real' Gene Kelly and Fred Astaire, now old men, take up the end of the ladder from the *That's Entertainment* number in the 1953 film **The Band Wagon**.

Not all forms that conserve Hollywood musicals are themselves films. Especially in the post-studio era, many living archives of MGM musicals assume a non-celluloid guise. TV musical-variety shows, to cite the most obvious case, frequently quote from Hollywood musicals in their production numbers. The now-defunct but widely syndicated **Carol Burnett Show** frequently based its 'tributes' and 'spoofs' on Hollywood musicals of the 1950s. The tribute will consist of song medleys or re-creations of numbers which

Astaire and Kelly take a nostalgic turn in **That's Entertainment, Part II**

104

fall within the realm of nostalgia; the spoofs also recreate numbers but in a way that exploits a mythical naive genre, exposing the remembered idiocies of earlier musical sagas.

When guest star Dick Van Dyke recreated Gene Kelly's *Singin' in the Rain*, it seemed at first a tribute, a quotation of the original. But due to Van Dyke's comic persona and the relative budgets of the two productions, an element of parody crept in. The

Table 2: Quotations from Hollywood Musicals (1960-80)

Same material	Different material
Inside Daisy Clover (1966) (source: MGM, Judy Garland)	TV: **The Carol Burnett Show** (1977) (source: **That's Entertainment**)
Finian's Rainbow (1968) (source: Fred Astaire)	**Donny and Marie** (1977) (source: Hollywood musical-production numbers)
A Clockwork Orange (1971) (source: **Singin' in the Rain**) **Une Femme est une femme** (Godard 1961) (source: MGM musical)	**Rainbow** (1978) (source: Judy Garland's early life as portrayed in Christopher Finch's biography)
The Boy Friend (1971) (source: Busby Berkeley)	Coffee-table books
Cabaret (1973) (source: backstage musicals)	'Making of' books Biographies of stars
Nashville (1975) (source: the backstage musical, **A Star is Born,** country music)	'Those Glorious MGM Musicals' original soundtracks
New York, New York (1977) (source: MGM musical, bandleader biopic)	**The Real McCoy** (Eliot Feld's ballet based on Hollywood musicals) **42nd Street** (smash 1980 Broadway musical based on the 1933 film)
The Wiz (1978) (source: **The Wizard of Oz**)	The MGM Grand Hotel, Las Vegas
All That Jazz (1979) (**A Star is Born**)	This book
Fame (1980) (source: Mickey Rooney - Judy Garland movies)	
Xanadu (1980) (source: **Cover Girl**)	

same **Carol Burnett Show** that season did a spoof on **That's Entertainment**. If the film itself (**That's Entertainment II**) implies that Astaire and Kelly are eternally youthful by having them do a few steps together, the spoof demystifies this claim, representing the dancers as senile old men in **That's Entertainment, Part 81**. The spoof gives us not re-creations of the original numbers but send-ups of the more ludicrous and campy aspects of our musical past — as in Carol Burnett's version of an Esther Williams water ballet. Yet both the bitter humor of the narrative segment and the gentle humor of the numbers stem from feelings of nostalgia towards the original objects.

Both those forms appearing to criticize the Hollywood musical and those appearing to eulogize it tend to move farther and farther away from the material of the 'original' sources. In the 1960s and 1970s the process of quotation and cancellation takes place on materials similar to the Hollywood musical and on materials quite different from celluloid musicals (see Table 2). In the case of the biographies, the narrative is the extra-filmic chronicle of the star's life. In the case of the coffee-table books, captions are placed under still photographs from the 'original' films. In the case of the production chronicles, the stories of the creation of the films are given alongside pictures and other memorabilia. In the case of the record-album reissues, the record jackets in both design and liner notes comment on the quoted material. Undoubtedly the most fanciful example of 'quotation' is the MGM Grand Hotel. Hollis Alpert has described the decor of that architectural spectacle in a way that renders its source material unmistakable:

The restaurants (the Gigi Room, for example, with French haute cuisine) echo the same theme — the grandness of MGM when Hollywood was in its star-studded prime. Twice each evening, hundreds of hopefuls line up in the monstrous lobby of the Grand on the chance of gaining entrance to the Ziegfeld Room and seeing the long-running 'musical extravaganza', Hallelujah Hollywood, *replete with long-stemmed show girls reminiscent of the chorus lines of MGM's vaunted musicals of the past. It's the most popular show in Las Vegas . . . the production numbers echo musicals such as* Meet Me in St Louis, The Pirate *and* Show Boat. ★

★ 'MGM: The Lion Finds New Game', **American Film**, vol.3 (February 1978) p.20.

As always, quotation implies the cancellation of the march of time. By recreating Hollywood musicals through quotation, Hollywood maintains its role as a living museum of entertainment, the bridge between folk art and the mass age of television.

Critical Reflexivity in
the Late Studio and Post-Studio Eras

Although a certain degree of remystification is inevitable in forms which are themselves examples of entertainment, a reflexivity which is far from conservative also enters into the later stages of a genre's development. Even those films which criticize older forms or stars only for rhetorical purposes nevertheless leave behind a residue of deconstruction, which sometimes lingers long after the happy ending has passed into the deeper recesses of our memory. While rejecting the concept of 'anti-musicals' (for all genres build in part through negation), it is still possible to examine recent musicals for contradictions and for elements of auto-critique within them. **Cabaret** was advertised as 'more than just a musical' as if everything preceding it had been somehow completely innocent. But we know that to be 'just a musical' is logically impossible.

When musicals do deconstruct, they tend to invert or negate previous generic hierarchies of values. It should not surprise us to find that what late musicals interrogate is their own basis in folk art. Self-criticism is most acute when attacking the cherished doctrine of spontaneity or when it shows an awareness of the role the internal audience plays, thus denying identification between the inside audience and the spectator.

In the MGM musical spontaneity reigned in the *bricolage* number, the very type of number that dominated **On the Town** and that subsequently comes under attack in Comden's and Green's sequel to **On the Town**, **It's Always Fair Weather**. In a kind of anti-

It's Always Fair Weather: *Situation-wise* and ...

107

number shocking for a 1950s MGM musical, Dan Dailey as a
disillusioned artist turned advertising executive hears ordinary speech
and starts to move to the beat of an inner band, just as Astaire and
Kelly did in countless situations. But now in *Situation-wise* Dailey's
movements express not a spontaneous receptivity to the music of life
but rather a kind of nervous tic. He is about to go berserk at the routine
his life has settled into. Dailey uses a lampshade and a towel to mimic
girls doing the Charleston; he simulates scenes from movies with
improvised props; he plays the bagpipes and fences; he attempts to
repeat a trick in which he removes a tablecloth without removing the
dishes only to have china crash to the floor in a symbolic breakdown.
Bricolage no longer represents a carefree life force; it assumes an inner
compulsion to destruction and chaos, qualities buried in the classical
musical's affirmation of liberation and personal energy. **Summer
Stock** had hinted at an anti-social tendency when the entertainers
destroyed the farmer's livelihood, the tractor. Now in Dailey's frantic
violence, destructive energy comes to the surface of the film in a quite
disturbing way. We begin to see the dangerous undercurrent to the
musical's wholehearted endorsement of spontaneous energy (of
course, the real equation between popular music and anti-social
violence would emerge in the rock culture of the 1960s).

    Situation-wise renders explicit the counter-conventional
forms the *bricolage* number may assume. Later in the same film,
spontaneity of performance itself comes under fire. We see a new
medium — television — exploiting the spontaneity of live trans-
mission to its own benefit. During a live 'This is Your Life'-type TV
broadcast, gangsters who are chasing Kelly break in and start a brawl

108

with the three heroes. Knowing the cameras are running, Kelly extracts a confession from the gangster. The cloying TV-show hostess turns to the camera and tells the audience that they have just been fortunate to witness 'a spontaneous and unrehearsed confession which will doubtless send him up the river for fifteen or sixteen years'. Now spontaneity is associated with the unsympathetic character and the unsympathetic medium (television).

Lili contests spontaneity as an all-embracing value to an even greater degree. Through the metaphor of a puppet show, Lili explores the musical's own need to provide performances which give an illusion of spontaneous evolution. The film imputes an unpleasant aura to MGM's merchandizing of the genuine and originally spontaneous qualities a star may possess. Lili (Leslie Caron) starts the film as a child-woman unable to distinguish real events from theatrical ones. She represents the ideal audience for any form of entertainment basing its appeal on illusionism (as did the MGM musical). The puppeteer (Mel Ferrer), recognizing Lili's naive belief in the reality of the puppets, revamps his carnival act around her. In making entertainment out of childish wonderment, he must teach Lili to adapt her spontaneous reactions to the needs of the audience, learning to project her voice when she talks to the puppets and wearing her child's costume as she strolls about the fairgrounds. Although the audience in the film sees only the presumably spontaneous show between Lili and the puppets, we see both the original evolution of the act and the marketing of it. We are witness to a montage of different versions of the act, each of them 'spontaneous'. We see Ferrer incorporating events from the offstage scenes into the act through his role as

Lili and her friends 'perform' for the audience in the film

spokesman for the puppets. This is true demystification; we know what the audience in the film does not know.

Yet in this blending of life and art, onstage and offstage, the manipulative and the ingenuous, it is impossible to say the act is either wholly spontaneous or wholly manipulative of its audience. The film becomes self-conscious about this in a scene where two entrepreneurs catch the puppet show and tell Ferrer:

> *You hit on a great idea combining the live figure with the puppets. We can't make up our minds whether she's a superb actress or you're a Svengali.*

Ferrer responds:

> *She lives each show. Her moments with the puppets are her happiest.*

This exchange calls into question the issue of manipulation — through spontaneity — in the musical itself. In **Lili** we are allowed to become cynical about the packaging of spontaneous performances only to have that cynicism called into question. **Lili** implies that just as it would be a mistake to discount the packaging, so would it be a mistake to decide too hastily that our pleasure in faked spontaneity is a pure product of manipulation. **Lili** implies that MGM took innately sincere stars like Judy Garland and merely presented them to us. A film produced the year after **Lili**, **A Star is Born**, would take a far more sober view of the studio as manipulator.

The Evolution of the Audience in the Film

Deductively, one could think of alternative uses for the audience in the film to the ones described in Chapter 2. Instead of using the internal audience to break down distance between moviegoer and performer by encouraging the moviegoer to take the point of view of an internal spectator, one could envisage ironic uses of audiences in films whereby the inside and outside audiences might be played in counterpoint. Needless to say, an ironic use of the inside audience did not catch on big during the studio era. ★ In recent years, however, the mindlessly applauding internal audience has been exposed in a variety of ways in several musical productions.

Woodstock would seem to represent the least radical use of the internal audience since, as a documentary of a 'real and spontaneous' event, the audience — in its sheer mass — really does become the spectacle. Not only may the spectator identify with the audience in the film, in many instances the spectator actually *was* in the film. Yet such a folk or quasi-folk event removes the screen of

★ In **The Work of Dorothy Arzner** (British Film Institute, 1975) Claire Johnston argues for a subversive reading of the 1940 Hollywood musical, **Dance, Girl, Dance**.

The audience in the film **Woodstock**

fiction from the classical musical, and in a sense, exposes the folk assertion all the more. The contradiction between the actual audience in the film and mass distribution was revealed to the author when spectators in Bloomington, Indiana, picketed the theater, refusing to pay admission to **Woodstock** *because they were in it*. The audience forced the exhibitor to make good on the bogus folk promise.

In the 1970s ironic comments on older entertainment practices became more and more common. Occasionally more specialized American television programs have even commented on the technological base of the medium itself (something that does not occur in 'family' programming, the present-day equivalent to the Hollywood musical). **The Paul Simon Special** (NBC, 8 December 1977) took for its format a *mise-en-abîme* structure in which the show is about the making of the show itself (a structure that has informed a number of American television specials). We are shown preparations, rehearsals, and some taping sessions for a show called 'The Paul Simon Special'. As in the Comden and Greene films, what we are shown is a demystification of the process of making — in this case — a taped television program. In one scene we see shots of applauding audiences being used to 'sweeten' the internal show. Simon makes fun of this by inserting into the tape of one of his numbers a totally unrelated shot of wildly applauding Chinese peasants. We even get the typical Comden and Green figure of the insincere-sincere entertainment personality (in this case a totally manipulative TV producer) who keeps urging Simon and Garfunkel to perform together (a reference to their well-known musical partnership). Just as the joke was never on Fred Astaire, the joke is now not on Simon and Garfunkel despite an

111

The political rally as spectacle — Nashville

added degree of irony and despite the extreme show of technology.

In two 'more than musical' films of the 1970s, the internal audience does seem to be used to implicate the spectator. **Cabaret** fades in on images of the decadent internal audience in a distorting mirror; it fades out on the same warped image of the internal audience with Nazi regalia fully visible. The implication is that we are seeing ourselves in that mirror. *Tomorrow Belongs To Me* sung by the German youth in a beergarden exposes the community song as a ritual of conformity. Audience participation becomes blind audience manipulation as the Germans rise one by one to pay tribute to Hitler's ideals. And yet, since we do not see ourselves on the movie screen, we may still distance ourselves from identifying with the audience in the film.

This is harder to do with **Nashville** which terminates in a singalong in which a mass audience is lulled into a celebration of its own complacency. Just in case we didn't identify with the crowd in the film, Robert Altman continues the music on the soundtrack long after the images have ended; the song itself goes: 'You may say that I ain't free, but it don't worry me'. And yet it seems likely that large segments of the actual audiences for these films saw the 'anti-musicals' as attacking someone other than themselves. It's easy to identify with the applause that greets a Fred Astaire number but it's hard to identify as mindless and manipulated sheep. Entertainment indicts its own audience at the risk of losing it.

Stars as Agents of Nostalgia

Perhaps more than any other type of studio film, the Hollywood musical was built around its singing and dancing stars. Gene Kelly might play an American in Paris in one film, a silent-movie idol in another, but when he danced, he always seemed to be 'Gene Kelly'. Little wonder the chief agents of demystification and nostalgia should be these same stars who aged along with the genre. Every time a star is mystified anew, the continuity of musical entertainment across generations is assured, as it is when Gene Kelly appears on television with Liza Minnelli or in a film with pop singer Olivia Newton-John. Two of these stars — Fred Astaire and Judy Garland — contributed to the genre's growth through demystification and regeneration. They will provide the final case studies of the historical processes at work in musical mass entertainment.

Fred Astaire

As part of a famous Broadway dance team (with his sister Adele), Fred Astaire had danced his way into many hearts before he came to the cinema. In his first screen appearance, in **Dancing Lady** (1933), Astaire plays himself, wandering into a rehearsal to dance with Joan Crawford as if the audience already knew who 'Fred Astaire' was. A Swiss number in the final show of **Dancing Lady** took its motif from *I Love Louisa,* a number in Astaire's 1929 Broadway revue, **The Band Wagon**. The same number, in a different setting, would again be

The making of the legend of Fred Astaire: **Dancing Lady** ...

associated with Astaire in the 1953 film **The Band Wagon**. The Astaire-Rogers series served to solidify in the minds of audiences an absolute identification of Fred Astaire with the dance.

Two signs of this identification pervade Astaire's films. The first is his trademark 'reflex' dancing in which his feet respond to the rhythm of the music independently of his conscious control. Involuntary dancing may be found in **Top Hat,** as when the amazed Astaire says to Ginger Rogers, 'Every once in while I suddenly find myself dancing'. In **Shall We Dance**, Astaire's dancing conforms to the speed of a record on his turntable. *Shoes With Wings On* in **The**

...and
Finian's Rainbow

114

Barkleys of Broadway has animated shoes coercing Astaire into the dance. And in his last dancing appearance, in **Finian's Rainbow**, Astaire tells Petula Clark he 'can't stop dancing'. The involuntary dancing motif not only serves to associate dancing with utterly spontaneous impulses; it also implies that for Astaire the dance is a life process, like breathing.

The involuntary motif connects Astaire's dancing to life; yet another conceit connects Astaire's dancing with salvation. Dance-song lyrics written for Astaire frequently use metaphors connecting dancing to heaven. In *Cheek to Cheek,* the very first beat of the song comes on the word 'heaven' making it the most emphasized lyric in the song. In another Irving Berlin lyric, achieving salvation is associated with Astaire's finding the right partner to dance with:

> It only happens when I dance with you
> That trip to **heaven** till the dance is through.

Even with a different lyricist, writing with Astaire in mind tended to produce the association with heaven. 'I'm up among the stars, on earthly things I frown', says Ira Gershwin's lyric to *I Can't Be Bothered Now.* Yet another Gershwin lyric, *Shoes With Wings On,* connects the dancer with angels, the most ethereal of creatures. The ultimate implication of a link between Astaire's dancing and salvation for the spectator occurs at the ends of **The Story of Vernon and Irene Castle** and **The Belle of New York** as Astaire and his partners go dancing off into the skies. Astaire may have imitated an angel in **Yolanda and the Thief** but in his 1950s musicals he becomes angelic himself.

Michael Wood describes Astaire's qualities as 'personal, universal, and apparently everlasting, exempt from history and geography', whereas he finds that Gene Kelly 'embodies a public, temporal, American promise'. ★ During the late 1940s and early 1950s the Astaire and Kelly personas interacted in such a way that Astaire was democratized and demystified. Increasingly Astaire would dance the kind of character roles associated with Kelly rather than portray a professional dancer. In **The Band Wagon**, Astaire is demystified by being presented as a washed-out hoofer only to be remythicized in making a comeback. In **Finian's Rainbow**, Astaire portrays an inelegant ragamuffin quite like the tramp he had portrayed *onstage* in *A Couple of Swells* (**Easter Parade**). Finian represents the inverse of Astaire's well-known screen figure. Yet as he dances off over the horizon at the end of the film, Finian is unmistakably Fred Astaire. As ever Astaire's demystification becomes his rebirth.

Astaire's films of the 1950s quote from Astaire's professional autobiography (which for the public was the only one that

★ Michael Wood,
**America in the
Movies**, p.148

mattered). **Easter Parade** alludes to Astaire's efforts to get a new partner after the break-up with Rogers. **The Barkleys** celebrates their reunion. **Royal Wedding** goes back to Astaire's original stage partnership with his sister Adele for its source. (Adele, like the sister in the film, left the act to marry British aristocracy.) **The Band Wagon** completely reassures the audience that Fred Astaire could never retire nor could his dance style ever appear dated. References to Astaire's career aid in the legendizing of his persona, stressing the length of his career, the continuity of his persona, and his importance to the audience.

Many of Astaire's films explicitly play a characteristic of the Astaire persona against their antithesis (represented by the woman). In **The Belle of New York** and **Silk Stockings**, the woman wholly accommodates her set of values to Astaire's. In **Silk Stockings**, Astaire comes to symbolize western capitalism, now associated with the values of entertainment: freedom, spontaneity, effortlessness. This is opposed to the rigid, militaristic mentality possessed in the film by Cyd Charisse's Ninotchka, and gradually abandoned, an abandonment marked by the sensuous dance in which she trades her military garb for silk and satin underwear. In **The Belle of New York**, Astaire is played off against yet another repressive work-oriented system — the Salvation Army — now represented by Vera Ellen. Astaire, as the devil-may-care playboy, attempts to get a job so that his Salvation Army love will dance with him. We are shown a montage sequence stressing the incongruity of Astaire in any uniform other than top hat, white tie and tails. Every job Astaire gets, he turns into a performance. A trolley car could never be anything but a platform on which to dance with Vera Ellen. By the end of his long career, Astaire had come to personify the values of the classical musical. It is not surprising that, in 1977, Astaire was introduced by a TV talk show host as *Mr Entertainment*.

The Belle of New York and **Silk Stockings** each contain numbers which appear to transcend their immediate narrative context and take on a larger significance. In **Silk Stockings**, Astaire's final solo to *The Ritz Roll and Rock* finds him in typical attire dancing to a Cole Porter parody of rock and roll. The number implies that Astaire may acknowledge changes in popular musical taste without ever being affected by them since he is above mere fashion and temporality. In **Belle**, in an attempt to win back Vera Ellen, Astaire takes a job as a singing waiter. At the restaurant, his number is announced and the curtain goes up to reveal Astaire — no longer in character — in a typical natty beige suit against a sky-blue backdrop. *I Wanna Be a Dancin' Man*, a sand dance with an utterly elegiac lyric, has nothing to do with the plot but everything to do with its anti-work ethic:

I wanna be a dancin' man while I can
Gonna leave my footsteps on the sands of time
If I never leave a dime....

Let other men build mighty nations and buildings to the
sky
I'll leave a few creations to show that I was dancing by.

I wanna be free as any bird can be (yes sir-ee)
Gonna leave my footsteps on the sands of time
If I never leave a dime.
A dancin' man with footsteps on the sands of rhythm and
rhyme.

Astaire breaks out of the character role to play his first and best screen role — himself dancing. There is no better example of the legendizing of Astaire within his films than this 1952 number which breaks out of the narrative in order to allow Astaire to pay tribute to his own art. Of all Astaire's solos, this was the one picked to introduce Astaire in **That's Entertainment Part II**. The number might have been written for a nostalgia film and, ironically, it fits better into the plot of **That's Entertainment** than it did into **The Belle of New York**. By the time Astaire dances off at the end of **Finian's Rainbow** he has already said goodbye enough times in enough films for his claim to immortality to be assured.

Judy Garland

★ Edgar Morin,
The Stars (New
York: Grove Press,
1960) p.37.

The star is not only an actress. The characters she plays are not only characters. The characters of her films infect the star. Reciprocally, the star herself infects these characters. ★

★ Christopher
Finch,
Rainbow: the
Stormy Life of Judy
Garland (New York:
Ballantine, 1975)
p.26.

Judy Garland's life was the basis for every performance she gave — good and bad — but it was Hollywood that provided her with her archetypal images: Dorothy, of course; the tramp, created for Easter Parade; the chic, androgynous vamp of her 'Get Happy' routine. To understand Judy Garland, one must try to understand Hollywood. ★

A Star is Born uses as source material not only Garland's MGM career but also events transpiring off the screen in the years since that career ended in 1950. Events surrounding Judy Garland's break with MGM, including a suicide attempt, gave the lie to Garland's wholesome, child-like screen persona. For the first time, the real facts of her life became known to the audience. In the early

1950s Judy Garland's MGM image was demystified then mystified through the agency of her comeback at the Palace Theater, New York, in 1951. 'Playing the Palace' had symbolized the ultimate synthesis of the couple and the show in **For Me and My Gal**. Garland's comeback show incorporated numbers from this and other MGM films, giving the act precisely the same nostalgia-evoking quality as the non-filmic sources in MGM musicals. Written by Roger Edens, directed by Charles Walters, Garland's Palace act opened with the lines:

> *I'm proud to play the Palace*
> *It's like a dream come true.*
> *That is why I want to shout it up and down*
> *Just to tell Broadway that the two-a-day is back in town.*

Garland's comeback could be considered another Freed Unit 'package', functioning to bring back the 'good old days' of vaudeville.

Both these events — the suicide attempt and the comeback — form the backdrop against which its original audience perceived **A Star is Born**. Within the film, broadly speaking, Judy Garland's real-life exposure to the public is represented by Norman Maine. But her Palace comeback is represented by Vicki Lester. This opposition between the death of the MGM musical and its resurrection permeates the film at other levels as well.

For example, the movement from Garland's first number (*Gotta Have Me Go With You*) to her second (*The Man That Got Away*) contrasts her old MGM image with her new tragic image. *Gotta* serves the function of exposing Norman's deterioration but also

The making of the legend of Judy Garland: **A Star is** Born echoes **Summer Stock** . . .

118

provides continuity between Judy Garland's last MGM number (*Get Happy* in **Summer Stock**) and her first reappearance on the screen in **A Star is Born**. Continuity of the persona is stressed both by her costuming (in both instances a man's tuxedo or suit jacket) and style of number and delivery (both are upbeat rhythm numbers backed by male choruses). The movement from this opening number to Garland's second number in the film, *The Man That Got Away,* parallels the movement from Garland's MGM persona to her exposure to the public. Singing becomes a means of expressing tragedy, heartbreak, alienation. The number incorporates Garland's new singing style with its histrionic excess and awkward gestures which would not have been tolerated at MGM. The motivation for *The Man That Got Away* is almost entirely extra-filmic. If one reads the film contextually, the number appears out of place; a tragic ballad of enormous intensity coming before anything has happened in the film. If one reads the number, however, as an acknowledgement of the MGM-Garland's demystification, its intensity seems far more understandable.

The same pattern of alternation between past and present occurs in the two set pieces of **A Star is Born,** both of which are parodies as well as reminders of MGM musicals. *Someone At Last* affectionately mocks MGM and the naïveté associated with Garland's MGM image (as when she says parenthetically, 'You know I get pretty girlish in this number'). *Born in a Trunk,* the long number within the film we see Vicki Lester making, perpetuates Garland's MGM image, yet undercuts the sentimentality by situating the number within an 'MGM musical' within the film. *Born in a Trunk* reprises Garland's own career, with references to her roots in vaudeville and to the Palace act (the recitative device and *Swanee*). Even though *Trunk* appears to parody MGM musicals — in particular the *Broadway Ballet* in **Singin' in the Rain** —it does not parody the 'sincere' Garland persona: indeed it sentimentalizes her. The final shot of **A Star is Born** in which a heavenly choir accompanies the camera craning further and further back from the triumphant 'Mrs Norman Maine' is perhaps the most mystifying shot in the entire history of the genre.

Although Judy Garland's later career served as a sad commentary on the 'decline' of the MGM musical, it was also one of the main forces keeping the public's memories of MGM musicals alive. Garland's later persona demystified the MGM musical but also created nostalgia for it since many of the numbers in her stage act were introduced in MGM musicals. Judy Garland's ritual singing of *Over the Rainbow* at the end of each stage performance served to evoke a sense of loss at the same time that it evoked warm memories of the innocence of Dorothy in **The Wizard of Oz**.

Garland's life has passed into popular mythology, epitomizing the failure of the vision of the MGM musical to extend into ordinary life. She has been the subject for novels such as **Valley of the Dolls**, and films such as **Inside Daisy Clover** about the exploitation of an adolescent singing star in the old Hollywood. Judy Garland died in 1969. It was not until 1974-5 that six biographical books appeared. ★ It would seem that enough time had elapsed for Garland herself to have come to represent the recently expired show-business past — now symbolized by the MGM musical. The 1979 TV season gave us **Rainbow**, a rather maudlin re-creation of the young Garland's exploitation by the studio. Already a sequel based on the star's adult career has been announced.

One would think all these exposés would tarnish Garland's legendary reputation as the greatest musical actress the cinema has yet produced. Precisely the opposite has happened.

New York, New York goes so far as to replace the MGM Garland persona with her own daughter, Liza Minnelli. The opening scene of **New York, New York** reprises Judy Garland's initial encounter with Gene Kelly in **The Pirate**. The plot of **New York, New York** reprises **A Star is Born**. Liza Minnelli's star being born serves to perpetuate the aura of the MGM musical, symbolized by both her famous parents. In his autobiography, Vincente Minnelli explicitly refers to the continuity of entertainment across generations. 'Her kind of talent comes along once in a generation', he says of Judy Garland, then goes on to ask the (for him) rhetorical question: 'Would it appear unseemly to suggest that Liza now wears that mantle?' ★ On a recent (1978) Gene Kelly television 'tribute' (**An American in Pasadena**) Liza

★ Vincente Minnelli, **I Remember it Well** (Garden City, New York: Doubleday, 1974); David Dahl, **Young Judy** (New York: Mason/Charter, 1975); Anne Edwards, **Judy Garland** (New York: Simon & Schuster, 1975); Gerold Frank, **Judy** (New York, Harper & Row, 1975); Hugh Fordin, **The World of Entertainment** (Doubleday, 1975); and Christopher Finch, **Rainbow**.

★ Vincente Minnelli, **I Remember It Well**, p.250.

120

Minnelli, not Judy Garland, is shown in flashback dancing to *For Me and My Gal* with Gene Kelly. Multiple diegesis is used to place past and present in the same frame, as in **The Band Wagon** insert into **That's Entertainment**. In this segment, the narrative consists of a sentimental visit by superstar Liza Minnelli to old family friend Gene Kelly's dressing room. They reminisce about the dance he and Liza had done on an earlier Kelly TV special. In a 'flashback' the color video image of the present-day narrative is framed in a box *inside* the black and white video image of young Liza and younger Gene Kelly. Near the end of their dance to *For Me and My Gal*, past and present, color and black and white video images are flipped with the past now framed inside the present. The TV show provides an almost uncanny example of the notion of the interchangeability of past and present entertainment forms and entertainment personas using a video musical to imply a film musical.

The Hollywood musical lives on in its star personas, symbols of the genre's vision and of the loss of that vision. The public's fascination with Judy Garland ten years after her death contributes to a continued interest in her films as well. The genre in a sense does not die; rather, it is transformed, and we must look to find it in unexpected places. Yet the more the genre is transformed, the more it remains the same. In 1975, Liza Minnelli talked to an interviewer

... and Judy at
Carnegie Hall

about the public's refusal to separate her from her mother both on and
offstage:

> *Do I have to talk about her any more? I don't know what else
> to say. Can't people accept that? How can they argue with that? Why
> do they want me to be the keeper of the flame and the destroyer of the
> myth at the same time?* ★

★ Barbara Grizzuti
Harrison, 'Liza
Minnelli Talks',
McCalls (May 1975)
p.125.

I would hope that this book has provided a framework for
answering such questions.

6:

A Postscript for the Nineties

The Hollywood Musical was very much a product of the intellectual atmosphere in film studies of the mid–late 1970s. That is to say it was influenced by the idea that spectators were positioned by the text, by Brechtian conceptions of modernism, and by structuralist notions of genre, even as it attempted to be more culturalist and more historical in its conception of the musical genre. At the same time, the idea of the musical was based on the classic Hollywood studio films; MTV did not go on the air until 1981; **Flashdance** was released in 1983. This chapter will therefore raise two related questions: do new developments in musical films of the 1980s challenge ideas based on more classical films; and, second, do new developments in cultural theory challenge the models for analysis employed in the first edition of this book? In answer to the first question, I will discuss the emergence of the teen musical as a 'postmodern' genre and as an example of the 're-construction' of the genre. In answer to the second question, I will discuss (in preliminary form) issues raised by subcultural theory and reception theory and try to relate them to shifting audience patterns. Indeed the historical backdrop for both forms of revisionism is the shift in the audience for musicals from a mass audience to specialized 'cult' audiences. Arguably the only form of musical that retains widespread popularity is the teen musical and even here the audience shifts to a large but circumscribed demographic group ('youth'). Cult audiences for musicals are more difficult to locate but arguably a large and identifiable one is the gay male urban subculture. The way this audience used and continues to use classic Hollywood musicals must lead to a different reading of the genre than that emphasized by Rick Altman, who overwhelmingly bases his model for the genre on ideas of normative (for the 1950s) heterosexual coupling. For Altman, to reject normative heterosexual coupling is to reject the genre; his theory does not explain how resisting readers may transform musicals.[1]

In short, part of the 'least common denominator' reading strategies of Altman's 'mass audience' involves an acceptance of what by the 1960s were already outmoded gender-based conventions of partnering. It is doubtful that this mass audience ever really existed even as a construct, for undoubtedly male and female audiences would have put different inflections on the generic heterosexual music man and his fair lady. But in applying a gay male paradigm to the text of heterosexual love, the definition of the Hollywood musical as based on heterosexual coupling is really interrogated. At another level, demographic changes challenge the model of the audience for musicals as a mass audience.

Since the 1950s but especially in the 1980s, the teenpic has been a dominant Hollywood film category, a mainstay for the profitability of the industry. However, it has received very little attention from theorists and critics, despite their interest in an ongoing debate over the nature of genre in film theory. Yet it seems to me that certain teenpics raise crucial issues for the continued relevance of genre studies to the field as a whole. Genre theory as applied to classic Hollywood studio films has been resolutely structuralist in its approach to the synchronic description of genres such as the Western, the musical and the detective film; and resolutely modernist in its description of the historical development of the genres. If we define genre as systematic intertextuality then film genre study has put the emphasis on systematicity and regularity at the expense of other possible more randomized, more fragmentary forms of intertextuality that have yet to be described.

A structuralist approach would seem to lend itself to the highly structured regularity both of studio-era films and modernist deconstructions of them. But the structuralist also tends to find regularity and binary thinking everywhere he looks (I use the pronoun intentionally to emphasize the masculinism of this approach). With the emergence of the teen film in the post-studio era, we are confronted by a different mode of production and a different manifestation of genre. The teen film may be described as a *postmodern* development within Hollywood genres, in that it presents fragmented, pastiche versions of older Hollywood genres. As literary critic Ralph Cohen points out in an article entitled 'Do Postmodern Genres Exist?', the very term 'genre' would appear to be incompatible with the term 'postmodern'. Cohen argues that the claim that postmodern writing blurs genres or transgresses them does not in itself inevitably invalidate all genre theories. Closer examination reveals the incompatibility exists only with certain older theories of genre: 'If we conceive of postmodernism as a style, it must be defined or described by being shown to be different from the modernist style. And yet any such change will inevitably call upon similarities or continuing features. If we conceive of postmodernism as a period, such description will have to include genres like tragedy or new mass culture genres like TV sitcoms and the detective or spy story and film.'[2]

The teen *musical* is not a genre in the sense that Thomas Schatz defines it in his book *Hollywood Genres*, that is, a community of interrelated character types.[3] Nor does it precisely fit Rick Altman's definition of genre as a set of semantic elements that coalesce into a stable syntax (pp.90–110). However, the 'teenpic', broadly speaking, may be considered a genre in both of these senses. Initially, the teen-pic emerged as one of the first examples of the post-studio mode of production in which a precise audience, in this case the youth audience, was 'targeted' for 'exploitation'.[4] This marked a break in marketing strategies from the 'least common denominator' targeting of the family audience that Altman considers crucial to the heyday of the Hollywood studio musical (p. 336). This shift in marketing strategy for the industry also coincided with the emergence of rock 'n roll which, as we shall see, led to different strategies for audiovisual representation as well. And yet the teenpic of the 1980s, because of its concern to exploit the youth audience, does develop a semantic lexicon as well as a syntax that stabilizes into a sexual coming-of-age narrative (e.g. **Risky Business, Fast Times at Ridgemont High, Ferris Bueller's Day Off**, and **Valley Girl**). The teen coming-of-age-comedy *is* a genre in the traditional sense with its semantics of the high school, the mall, the sex-crazed teen male, the boy-crazed teen females, etc. We can even follow Altman's distinction between teenpics that are primarily semantic and those that are syntactic. For example the Western **Young Guns** has none of the semantics of the teenpic but preserves the syntax of the adolescent male group, one that combines readily with the Western. And many horror films have a teenpic semantics, whether in terms of setting (**Heathers** – the high school) or the community of teenpic character types, without sharing the maturation narrative or comic plot of the typical teen comedy.

Generic evolution

Film genre studies and structuralism enjoyed so close a bond in the 1970s that they appeared to be one and the same. Since genres presumably are systems, rather than individual artifacts, it would seem that a structuralist approach would be inevitable; however, the structuralist approaches that followed Lévi-Strauss repeated his pattern of emphasizing synchronic regularities. The synchronic emphasis is redoubled when genre theorists go on to describe the 'evolution' (Schatz) or 'transformation' (Cawelti) of genres.[5] What you get is basically a transformation from one synchronic system to another – either the later genre films systematically render self-conscious the classical genre or they demythologize it or they critique or deconstruct it. The late genre film then becomes a modernist re-writing of the classical genre.

My own theory of generic development stressed this kind of movement toward what I called critical reflexivity. Although I also talked about a conservative or constructive reflexivity that operates historically within the musical genre, I was primarily interested in an increasingly more apparent use of self-reflexive techniques at the end of the studio era and after; therefore, I saw modernist self-reflexivity in the late studio and post-studio era musical as a dialectical process in which each deconstructive move served to maintain the genre but also each new construction had a deconstructive edge. In this way self-reflexive musicals are 'modernist' in that they systematically deconstruct those very elements that give the genre its regularity. For example, the rehearsal number Garland does in **A Star is Born** (1954) systematically debunks the principle of the spontaneous generation of performance in musicals.

In order to illustrate the strategy of modernist re-writing, I would like to discuss **Pennies from Heaven** (1981) as the furthest development of this tendency. Based on a British television six-part series by Dennis Potter, this film seemed destined to fulfill the prophecy of the first edition of this book. However, my predictive powers are questioned by the amazing success of the 1987 film **Dirty Dancing**, the best example of what I will term the 'reconstructive' tendencies of teen musicals.

Pennies from Heaven may be described as modernist and even as Brechtian, but it does not take a *Screen* theorist to apply this label to the film. Pauline Kael does it in her 1981 review. She writes, 'Despite its use of Brechtian devices, **Pennies from Heaven** doesn't allow you to distance yourself.'[6] Clearly the mass audience which avoided this film in droves disagreed. No better example exists of what Brecht himself called 'the separation of the elements'. In his preface to *Mahagonny*, Brecht writes,

> *When the epic theatre's methods begin to penetrate the opera the first result is a radical* separation of the elements. *The great struggle for supremacy between words, music and production – which always brings up the question 'which is the pretext for what?': is the music the pretext for the events on the stage, or are these the pretext for the music? etc. – can simply be by-passed by radically separating the elements. So long as the expression 'Gesamtkunstwerk' (or 'integrated work of art') means that the integration is a muddle, so long as the arts are supposed to be 'fused' together, the various elements will all be equally degraded, and each will act as a mere 'feed' to the rest. The process of fusion extends to the spectator, who gets thrown into the melting pot too and becomes a passive (suffering) part of the total work of art. Witchcraft of this sort must of course be fought against. Whatever is intended to produce hypnosis, is likely to induce sordid intoxication, or creates fog, has got to be given up.* Words, music and setting must become more independent of one another.[7]

The sound–image relationship in **Pennies from Heaven** exemplifies the 'distancing effect' that comes from separating the elements. When, instead of singing the numbers in the film, the characters lip-sync to old recordings from the 1930s, we are rendered

Using old recordings:
Pennies from Heaven

aware of the constructed nature of the text rather than 'hypnotized', 'intoxicated', or 'fogged' out. This separation of the elements also seems to represent a critique of the traditional use of diegetic music in the musical genre. The idea that one spontaneously, naturally sings is exposed through this technique. Although we will also see a move toward non-diegetic music in the teen musicals, it is the specifically modernist Brechtian tendency that I am noting here.

Intertextuality in **Pennies from Heaven** also works in a modernist way. The film quotes widely from its musical comedy heritage, favoring 1930s traditions contemporary with the film's setting, as when Berkeleyesque chorines invade a bank and schoolchildren tap and play violins. The most extreme case of quotation occurs near the end of the film, when, fleeing the cops, the couple hide out in a movie theater screening Astaire and Rogers in *Let's Face the Music and Dance* from **Follow the Fleet**. Although in the original film this borderline camp number gets away with its excess by being located within a show, **Pennies** chooses not to provide the show-within-a-film context, taking the number instead for its Depression-era combination of glamour and despair, its motif of transcendence through dancing. As the scene in **Pennies from Heaven** progresses, it becomes clear that its purpose is critique, not nostalgia or pastiche. Initially, Arthur utters clichés as they view: 'There's gotta be something on the other side of the rainbow.' And Eileen responds in kind: 'There always is.' They watch Astaire do the song; Arthur starts to lip-sync to Astaire, addressing the lyric of hope amidst despair to Eileen. When we see the screen again, Arthur and Eileen appear as tiny figures in front of the massive images of Astaire and Rogers. They begin to mime the dance, step for step, but after a cutaway to a male

Quoting from 1930s musicals: **Pennies from Heaven**

128

chorus (à la **Top Hat**) we cut back to reveal Eileen and Arthur replacing Fred and Ginger on the silver screen, now inside the diegesis of a film text that becomes increasingly different from the original number. They dance but are surrounded by a chorus in top hat and canes who become increasingly more menacing until the canes take the form of prison bars closing over the doomed couple. Outside the theater, Arthur has lost the illusion; although Eileen does a few bars of *Singin' in the Rain*, they are wanted for murder.

Not only does the use of quotation have a critical function, but also **Pennies from Heaven** illustrates what Rick Altman means when he says that late musicals represent a 'return to the semantic genre' (p. 270). If we consider **Pennies** to be a deconstruction of Altman's folk sub-genre, we find that every element of folk semantics from the classical period is present in the film. Arthur and his wife's bourgeois Chicago home and Eileen's farmhouse provide an emphasis on family groupings and the home; Galena, Illinois, 1934, provides the small-town or agricultural setting; the sets are based on conventions of American Depression-era painting (Edward Hopper's *Nighthawks*) and documentary photography; amateur performance is emphasized (none of the characters is a professional); and no one would question that a serious or melodramatic tone prevails. And yet the way these semantic elements are combined – what Altman calls their syntax – regularly inverts the classic sub-generic syntax; for instance, Altman says of the folk musical, 'The sounds of nature inspire man to make music.' In **Pennies from Heaven**, not even old musicals inspire the characters to make their own music. Altman writes, 'One of the lovers represents the stability of the earth, the other energy and movement.' This would seem to be true of **Pennies**. She's a small-town school-marm; he's a travelling salesman, but the syntax is rendered problematic by the fact that he's already married to someone else (Altman, pp. 273–315).

My point is that the modernist musical *systematically* deconstructs the classic syntax of the genre. **Pennies from Heaven** is thus the film that seemed almost uncannily to fulfill the developmental theory which I sketched in the first edition. But this theory did not anticipate a development within the musical genre that was intertextual but neither deconstructive nor self-reflexive.

This is precisely where the teen musical comes into play. Tag Gallagher has criticized evolutionary theories of generic development by arguing that the historical development of genres is cyclical not linear.[8] This would certainly seem to be true of the musical. Instead of moving progressively from an experimental, transparent or naive conception of its material to an increasingly more self-reflexive mode, the American film musical appears to have returned to its infancy with the new teen musicals of the 1980s. But this cyclical development is neither random not ahistorical. It's a result of shifting industrial and audience patterns. What's wrong with an evolutionary theory of development is that it is ahistorical and teleological. I believe it is entirely appropriate to look at the musical genre in terms of historical development. I also believe that the teen musical represents a new stage of that development, a tendency that needs to be differentiated from the critical, modernist extremes of **Pennies from Heaven**.

If as Altman also argues (p. 251), the musical has to reach a new audience – young people rather than a family audience – how did it adjust to accommodate this new audience? I will argue that the teen musicals of the 1980s represent a 'reconstruction' in the sense that they are not parodic or deconstructive of the conventions of the classic musical. Rather, they introduce new conventions – the main one being the use of 'non-diegetic' rock music over the images rather than the use of diegetic music that defined the older form of musical film. But teen musicals are not a new genre: they also maintain in fragmented form many of the mainstays of the classical Hollywood musical – including the three major narrative patterns described by Altman – the show, the fairytale and the folk. Thus what I am describing represents a postmodern development of a genre as opposed to the modernist evolution toward deconstruction described by previous genre theorists.

As opposed to the modernist film which illustrates semanticity with a reversal of syntax, in **Dirty Dancing** all of Altman's sub-genres can be argued to be present in the film in a kind of pastiche. The folk musical is present in the semantics of the emphasis on the nuclear family and the nostalgic locale of a real American ethnic setting, in this case the Catskills of 1963. The combination of old with new music written specifically for the film is just as true of **Dirty Dancing** as it was for **Meet Me in St Louis**. There is a strong emphasis on amateur performance; in fact, the film culminates in an amateur talent show. Traces of Altman's fairytale sub-genre are also present. The characters travel to an unreal setting represented by a hotel, as in **Top Hat**. Most significantly, the fairytale syntax is present in the class differences between the couple. Altman says of the fairytale musical, 'she is a foreign princess, he is a commoner' (p. 152). In this case, she is a Jewish American Princess; he is a working-class 'hunk'. The classic show musical is incorporated at the level of syntax. The film ends with the classic show syntax of the couple coming together in and through a musical performance. But in folk fashion, it is a performance that galvanizes Kellerman's dying resort community into a singing and dancing mass. The idea that dancing together brings about falling in love is classic. Also the idea that he *creates* art, she *is* art, is present in

He teaches her to dance; she teaches him middle-class values. Cynthia Rhodes, Jennifer Grey and Patrick Swayze in **Dirty Dancing**

the tried and true motif of the man teaching the woman to dance and, thereby, creating her as an object of spectacle. Yet **Dirty Dancing** can also be read according to Altman's dual-focus model: the repressed of each returns as the surface of the other. Johnny becomes idealistic and assertive; Baby gets in touch with her sexuality.

But none of these uses of the classic sub-genre is deconstructive. None represents the separation of the elements called for by Brecht. In fact, these sub-generic elements represent a form of random quotation and pastiche that makes the film pleasurable in all the ways that Brecht would have disapproved of. The 'witchcraft' of **Dirty Dancing** is intended to produce hypnosis and *is* likely to induce sordid intoxication. The main reason that teen musicals have not been considered musicals is the absence of diegetic singing in them, although diegetic dancing is quite common. The idea that the story is told through the numbers is an element of the classic musical that seems definitional to some. But the use of pre-recorded music in **Dirty Dancing** in no way represents a separation of the elements. Everything is done to link the pre-recorded songs to the diegesis. In most of the numbers, the non-diegetic music is at least thematized, or it is rendered diegetic by being played on a phonograph within the scene. The climactic number in which Johnny reappears to dance with Baby in the final show commemorates their summer together with the song *I Had the Time of My Life*; at one point Johnny appears almost to sing the lyric to Baby. This represents, not separation, but fusion into a new set of conventions more palatable to the teen audience than those of the classic musical. After all, if the 'folk' of the pre-World War II era produced their music around the family piano, arguably dancing or singing along or combing one's hair to pre-recorded music captures the daily experience of the walkman generation.

In this regard, the music video is the ultimate 'postmodern musical' taking to an extreme the fragmentation of narrative. Despite the emphasis on performance in most music videos, however, and despite individual instances of pastiche, music videos cannot be considered musicals if we define the musical by its dual levels of narrative and number. In the music video, everything is subordinated to the song, even the running time. In this sense, videos are more like commercials for musicals than like classic Hollywood musicals. Certain music videos have links to or quote from previous or contemporary musicals. **Flashdance**, for instance, pioneered the film/video tie-in with videos based on the diegesis of the film; **Dirty Dancing** cashed in on this successful pattern with both videos and soundtrack recordings.[9] The Janet Jackson video 'All Right' featured a surprise appearance by Cyd Charisse in front of a movie marquee. And of course the over-analysed Madonna video 'Material Girl' pastiches both the *Diamonds are a Girl's Best Friend* number and certain narrative tendencies from Marilyn Monroe's **Gentlemen Prefer Blondes**. What MTV lends to the reconstructive teen musical is a new way of organizing the sound/image relationship that may be adapted to feature-length films which otherwise maintain the narrative/number distinction. That is to say, the 'numbers' may be structured around a non-diegetic popular song to which the characters dance or throughout which narrative segments of an episodic structure are rhythmically cut. Although this is by no means an original idea (think of the *Raindrops* montage in **Butch Cassidy and the Sundance Kid**, 1969), the vogue for MTV in the 1980s created an acceptance of this new convention.

The more successful teenpic musicals appear to have followed the reconstructive pattern of **Dirty Dancing**: **Flashdance**, **Footloose**, and **Hairspray** are examples. These films have restored the classic

Flashdance:
everybody dances,
even a street cop

syntax of Hollywood musicals while realigning in pastiche fashion elements of subgeneric syntax and semantics. **Flashdance**, for example, was widely criticized for its narrative incongruities (a woman steelworker living in a trendy loft in Pittsburgh becomes a ballet dancer) yet when viewed as a reconstructive musical, its fragmentation (oddly enough) seems more an attempt at a new unity. Fragments from the folk musical (everybody dances, even a street cop) combine with a typical fairy-tale plot (working-class girl falls for rich factory-owner) to culminate in the ultimate show finale. After auditioning (successfully we are led to believe) for the ballet, the music from the audition (*What a Feeling*) moves out into the world as the love plot is resolved with the now prima ballerina offering a rose to her real-life partner. As ever, a show is a metaphor for love; and love is what makes a 'show' happen. As contemporary, as video-like, as ad-like as **Flashdance** seemed in 1983, its basic narrative pattern was as old as the musical itself (and older still when traced back to its literary and theatrical roots).

Similarly, the teen musical **Footloose** could be viewed as a remake of **Dames** (1934) with a small-town setting and without Dick Powell's diegetic crooning. Although all of the numbers are episodic sequences with the music over the visuals, the film is a typical musical in that each number is structured around a song that refers to the narrative either directly or thematically; and in its motif of the glorification of the dance. Directed by Herbert Ross[10], **Footloose** opens with a quotation from **Top Hat** in the motif of images of dancing feet under a song about dancing feet (the title song). The youth vs. Puritanism thematics are introduced as a church sermon, condemning 'obscene rock n' roll music', is greeted by a teen girl applying nail polish. As in **Dames**, an organized, religiously and legally authorized

133

adult vigilante group is pitted against the subversive youthful energy of kids who want to dance. And as in **Dames**, youth eventually wins out, the show goes on, and the Puritanical adults are re-energized by the forces of entertainment. As with **Summer Stock**, whose folk semantics are eventually inscribed within a successful Broadway show, **Footloose** begins by opposing dancing and community values, but ends with a merger between the values of community and the values of entertainment. As in the 1950 film, the rural community sees dancing as dangerous, ostensibly because a group of teens died in an auto-accident after a dance, but really because, as the preacher/parent tells his wife, 'when kids dance together, they become sexually irresponsible'. The boy who wants to dance gives a speech in front of the town council linking dancing to community and even religious values. The film is resolved by redefining dance away from sexuality and towards 'celebrating life'. The speech authorizes dancing in the Bible; 'this is our time to dance', the boy says. Ultimately the preacher/father of the reckless, sexually promiscuous girl gives the Lord's blessing to a high school dance with which the film culminates. Dancing not only proves to be a responsible way of channeling the young folks' sexual energy, it also rejuvenates the parents' marriage.

The Roger Corman-produced **Rock 'n' Roll High School** (1979), which at first glance appears more teenpic than musical, taps

into this apocalyptic vein in the musical and teenpic genres that links popular music to youthful sexual energy. But instead of channeling that energy in socially acceptable directions, the film ends with the teenagers burning down their school to the beat of the Ramones. **Rock 'n' Roll High School** draws on conventions of the classic musical in order to subvert them rather than for the purposes of recombination as in the more commercial films. The fact that **Footloose** and **Rock 'n' Roll High School** may both be classified as postmodern teen musicals raises thorny issues of generic classification. Since almost all teenpics contain rock music (either diegetic or on the soundtrack or both), the boundaries between the teenpic and the teen musical are blurry; it is difficult to specify when a teen film becomes a musical. Although I want to look at teen films that actually seem to continue traditional genres, specifically those that seem to represent a new kind of Hollywood musical, I fully admit that when faced with a postmodern genre, principles of selection become problematic. For example, a film such as **Footloose** fits every definition of the teenpic genre – it has the community of interrelated character types as well as a high school semantics and a theme that links music/dancing to anarchic rebellion against authority. In this sense, it does not differ from say, **Rock 'n' Roll High School**, one of the great cult teen films, which culminates in the rebellious students burning down the school. Yet I have classified **Footloose** as a teen *musical*.

There are a number of ways of dealing with this distinction, each of which has consequences for the way we conceptualize the teen musical. To use Rick Altman's distinction, **Rock 'n' Roll High School** is a semantic musical in that it shares some specific traits with classic musicals: the presence of diegetic music, the association of music with youthful anarchy, the presence of various 'shows' in the narrative. But the film is not a syntactic musical: it does not have a couple who

135

exchange sets of values; the diegetic music does not characterize each half of the couple; and most significantly, the show at the end does not form a new couple in a new community. The ending is more like that of the show musical in which the values of entertainment triumph over the Puritan ethic. But the entertainment values which triumph are those of an anti-social anarchy rather than a recuperable pleasure. The semantic genre/syntactic genre distinction, while useful up to a point, does not account as well for films which veer off from the classic musical values into more ideologically suspect or radical directions, and yet which are not in a Brechtian modernist vein either.

Other teenpic musicals have taken this more deconstructive path; none of them have been mainstream commercial teen films, however. **Absolute Beginners**, which quotes extensively from Hollywood musicals even to the point of turning Soho into the MGM back lot, goes so far as to make cynical references to **The Wizard of Oz**. Yet even this film, very similarly to **Pennies from Heaven** (both are British in origin), resorts to a Brechtian version of the classic happy ending, as does John Waters' more avant-garde follow-up to **Hairspray**, the box-office failure **Cry Baby**. Each film ends with an abrupt transition from (racial) conflict or chaos to the traditional final embrace by the young couple. **Hairspray**, while fully 'culinary'[11], also deconstructs many of the building blocks of Hollywood musicals, especially in terms of racial, gender and body-image stereotypes. The heroine is a self-affirming fat girl, the triumph of entertainment includes black youths, and the usually puritanical parental figure is played by Divine in drag. Although not marketed as a 'teen musical' or teenpic, Spike Lee's **School Daze** uses musical production numbers of a more conventional kind, with on-screen singing and dancing. Spike Lee uses certain conventions of musicals to arouse expectations in the audience which he then frustrates. About twenty minutes into the film, he stages a big production number that in true musical style sets up a dual-focus opposition between the 'Straight and Nappy'. The stylized dance number echoes back and forth between the Gamma Rays, light-skinned women with 'good hair', and the independents, dark-skinned women with 'bad hair' in this campus film about Black college life. Although this number cues us to expect a classic musical structure, no more such abstract numbers occur in the film; the remaining musical performances are motivated by context. According to Maureen Madison, 'by couching a thought-provoking, political and racially innovative film in the semantics of the musical genre, Spike Lee frustrates all expectations and tests the capacity of any spectator's ability to establish meaning'.[12]

Rather than dismissing these films as mere 'semantic' musicals or seeing them as modernist where they are not, it might be better to

Colleen Fitzpatrick,
Debbie Harry, Divine
and Ricki Lake in
Hairspray

consider the postmodernism of these teen musicals in a different light than the postmodernism of the more ideologically conventional films. Linda Hutcheon has made the useful distinction that postmodern art is both complicitous and critical.[13] Unlike modernist art, it does not critique from a position outside consumer culture; yet it may critique from a position of complicity within that culture. In the case of teen musicals, rather than asking whether or not they are really musicals, we might learn more by distinguishing those films or parts of films that lean toward complicity and those which lean toward critique, while acknowledging that all the films contain both poles. In this way, we are reinstating the demystification/remystification dialectic within a postmodern rather than modernist frame. Teen musicals may acknowledge their debt to Hollywood while at the same time distancing themselves from the old conventions.

Interestingly two abysmal failures – the film **Lambada** (1990) and the TV series **Hull High** (first broadcast 20 August 1990) – completely misunderstood the importance of the couple/show syntax as a link to successful musicals of the past. **Lambada** attempted to exploit the dance craze by linking it to a teenpic narrative in which a high school math teacher tutors disadvantaged youth at a dance hall. But the dance craze is not linked to the couple – in this regard the producers could have benefited from a screening of **The Gay Divorcee** – and the love plot, according to which a high school student attempts to seduce her married math teacher, prevents the establishment of a couple at all. Attempts to adapt the musical form to television have had to confront the problem of the strong thrust toward closure that the couple/show syntax lends to the musical film. The television series format, with its weak episodic closure, tends to lack energy. The teen TV series **Fame** (1982–87), based on the 1980 teen musical, motivated most individual episodes by a focusing of communal energy on a final show of one kind or another; even so, it lacked the exciting finale of the film and tended more toward teen melodrama than teen comedy. The US TV series **Hull High** failed to adapt the teen musical to television in the same season that Steven Bochco's much-publicized **Cop Rock** failed to integrate the cop show with the musical. The first episode of **Hull High** uses rappers as narrators (a clever way of eliminating the Black performers from the plot line) in a plot typical of the male-oriented teenpic. The male gaze of both students and teachers focuses on the sexy English teacher whose 'hot' dance number is positioned as a male sexual fantasy (she even tells her male colleague 'I need you to watch me'); meanwhile a nerdy girl student has a nerdy boy student photograph her in the nude in the boys' locker room. Thus **Hull High** managed to be both racist and sexist. The series ignored the 1980s development of the female-centered teenpic (e.g. **Sweet Talk**, **Pretty in Pink**, **Heathers**, **Shag**, **Where the Boys Are**, **Rock 'n' Roll High School**, **Valley Girl**, **Fast Times at Ridgmont High**, **Modern Girls**), a format that dominated the 1980s teen musical (e.g. **Girls Just Want to Have Fun**, **Hairspray**, **Flashdance**, **Dirty Dancing**). Although the classic Hollywood musical did have a long tradition based on the gaze of the male spectator at the female chorus girl, the genre appealed heavily to a female audience and its dominant impulse, as Altman so thoroughly shows, was toward a dual focus narrative in which male and female viewpoints alternated. The male-centeredness of the typical 'boy' teen film (**Risky Business**, **Ferris Bueller's Day Off**, etc.) with its emphasis on the sexual conquest of the girl as part of the path to manhood, does not lend itself to a structure of duality. Although it was a 'real' musical with production numbers, the early demise of **Hull High** can scarcely be regretted. The linking of musical numbers with a comic plot has proven highly resistant to change, at least for films and series aimed at the young adult audience. In this sense, at least, my analysis of the power of this classic pattern holds up well.

Gay Readings

The first edition of this book ended on a freeze-frame of Judy Garland as the archetypal figure for the dynamics of demystification and remystification in the classical Hollywood musical. For me Judy epitomized both the failure of the musical to penetrate everyday life and the dream of doing so that made the genre popular. This imagery of tragedy and hope, Kansas and Oz, breakdown and comeback has also formed the basis for Judy's cult status in the urban gay male subculture.[14] Thus it is not surprising that the initial work on this subculture's involvement with musicals has taken the form of Garland studies. I do not use this term facetiously. The depth of fan scholarship on Garland is impressive, culminating perhaps in the recently published reference work, *The Complete Judy Garland*. Of this encyclopedia Ethan Mordden has written that it is 'detailed to the point of dementia: an appendix without a book ... the wealth – or, at any rate, the amount – of data is staggering. Still, the very appearance of such books, from major publishers, tells us how primary Garland remains in the culture.' Mordden's disapproving tone seems curious, since it is made within the pages of a lengthy and detailed Garland career analysis.[15] Richard Dyer brilliantly shows us how the gay subcultural reading of Garland based on her later career leads to a retrospective reading of her MGM films not available to contemporary audiences. And Janet Staiger describes attempts to reconstruct the meaning of Garland prior to **A Star is Born** to see if gay audiences already read the tragedy of her life into the comedy of her films. This by no means indicates that the gay cult interest in Judy is marginal to our understanding of the *dominant* strategies of the musical genre; although they displace the heterosexual couple from the center of the genre, gay readings of Garland are central to the thematics of the genre described in the first edition of this book; the Garland legend figures prominently in Altman's account of the genre as well. In this way *all* readings of Garland *vis à vis* the musical genre are 'queer readings' in the sense Alexander Doty implies:

> *My use of the terms 'queer readings', 'queer discourses,' and 'queer positions,' then, are attempts to account for the existence and expression of places within culture, cultural production, and cultural reception that are 'queer' or 'different' and which can't fully, clearly, or accurately be articulated through heterosexual positions and discourses – or, again, sometimes even by the range of gay and lesbian positions and discourses. I am using the term 'queer' in cultural studies to*

mark a flexible space for the expression of all aspects of non-straight cultural production and reception. As such, this cultural 'queer space' recognizes the possibility that various and fluctuating (queer) positions might be occupied whenever anyone [italics in original] produces or responds to culture.[16]

The emphasis (thus far) on gay men's relationship to Judy Garland could usefully broaden out to include gay readings of the musical genre as a whole from the triple perspectives of 'queer' authorship of musicals, a 'queer sensibility' to be read from the films and studies of actual gay male readings of musicals that have been or might be made.

What might a reinterpretation of the musical from a gay subcultural perspective look like? For one thing, we must examine the question of gay authorship. According to Alexander Doty, the attribution of gay authorship to a text is important because 'knowledge of the biographies of both director and spectator can become crucial to constructing queer discourses within auteurist positions'.[17] What happens when, for instance, the Freed Unit at MGM gets rewritten as 'the fairy unit', the phrase heterosexual producer Arthur Freed jokingly used to refer to his unit? According to Garland biographer Christopher Finch, 'It has already been noted that the Freed Unit included a sizable gay contingent .... The many gifted homosexuals who worked on his films were to a considerable extent responsible for the mood and spirit of the musicals he produced, and for the social ambiance that surrounded their making. Judy was totally at home with this group, sharing both its sensibility and its sense of humor.'[18] The attribution of gay authorship to Freed Unit musicals and to musical films in general enables us to conceptualize musicals as gay male texts created by and addressed to gay men. It also authorizes a reading of Judy Garland as knowingly 'queer' and 'camp' in her own sensibility. But this gay subtext needs to be read from beneath the dominant heterosexual text (for of course MGM musicals were *supposed* to be addressed to a family audience). Gay authorship does not in itself necessitate a gay reading of the text; but in the case of musicals it can be used to reinforce the idea (expressed by Finch, Dyer and others) that musicals express a gay sensibility, especially in their embodiment of camp.

The issue of a gay sensibility informing the work of directors such as Vincente Minnelli and Busby Berkeley centers on issues of camp and spectacle. Dyer quotes Jack Babuscio and Vito Russo to show that the idea of a gay sensibility is based on the theatricality of having to pass as straight in everyday life and of the risks (symbolized for Russo in Garland's performances) involved in presenting oneself to the world. Dyer goes on to suggest that the 'gay sensibility' 'holds together intensity and irony, a fierce assertion of extreme feeling with a deprecating sense of its absurdity'.[19] This sensibility finds expression in the aesthetic of camp which in turn provides a link between a subcultural 'structure of feeling' and certain ways of reading musicals. 'Queer' readings of musicals would shift the emphasis from narrative resolution as heterosexual coupling (an emphasis on the comic plot) and toward readings based on non-narrative, performative and spectacular elements (an emphasis on the numbers). Such readings might also reinterpret musical narratives away from the emphasis on the comic plot as a form of closure that reconfirms heterosexual cultural norms.[20] An archetypal camp Busby Berkeley text, **The Gang's All Here**, for example, has the script of a perfectly average World War II 'troop show' musical. Were it not for the spectacular and bizarre production numbers along with the presence of Carmen Miranda, the film would not maintain its premier place in the camp canon; ditto with the swimming spectaculars of Esther Williams, parodied by Carol Burnett and others. The presence of these camp figures in the films renders the entire film subject to a camp reading. In the case of **The Gang's All Here**, the high camp of Miranda's onstage numbers carries over to permit a parodic reading of the heterosexual couple formed by Alice Faye and 'Sergeant Casey aka Andy Mason', as well as the 'couple' formed by Edward Everett Horton and Eugene Pallette. Another high camp moment in the history of musicals occurs in **Thrill of A Romance**, when Esther Williams teaches prospective partner Van Johnson to swim, and he imitates her ultra-femme backstroke as they cover the pool in perfect sync. In this sense camp figures such as Carmen Miranda would assume a greater role in the history of the genre; but major stars such as Garland, Kelly and Astaire may also be rearticulated around specifically gay discourses. During the heyday of Hollywood musicals, for example, the status of the male dancer as a heterosexual figure was always in question; in the case of Kelly and especially the non-macho Astaire, heterosexuality had to be asserted; it could not be assumed. How would this influence a reading of the films by both gay and straight audiences? What about the oft-reproduced rehearsal photo of Fred Astaire twirling in his arms his own male double Hermes Pan?

How would the assumption of a gay male audience change, for example, my reading of classic Minnelli musicals such as **Yolanda and the Thief** and **The Pirate**? Above all, a gay subcultural reading would elevate these two Minnelli masterpieces of the 1940s above the currently more esteemed Freed Unit musicals of the 1950s -- **Singin' in the Rain** and **The Band Wagon**, whose sophistication stems more from their smart Comden and Green scripts than from elements of excess in their *mise-en-scène*. The gay reading would thus emphasize different aspects of the films: the 'look' over and above the narrative codes in a film such as **Yolanda**, whose ending is the most conventional example of the wedding dissolve. That is to say, whereas Altman would read the ending of **Yolanda** as dominant in its formation of the married heterosexual couple, the gay reading would stress the wild exaggeration of the *mise-en-scène* throughout and might even ignore the ending, as Elizabeth Ellsworth says lesbian readers ignored the heterosexual ending of **Personal Best**.[21] **Yolanda** gives us a camp masquerade of conventional heterosexual courtship with Fred Astaire's character impersonating an angel and Lucille Bremer's Yolanda impersonating a naive virgin. The film leaves afterimages of the scarlet robes of the convent students and the undulating black and white floor of the *Coffeetime* number; from the perspective of camp, the wedding finale itself may appear to be a parody of the typical musical closure, as the stunned (and thus apparently still monogamy-shy) Astaire gets a glimpse of his enormous future family.

For Dyer **The Pirate** is the ultimate test of Garland's camp status; of her MGM films 'only **The Pirate** seems to use Garland's campness in a sustained fashion in its play with sex roles and spectacular illusion, two of the standard pleasures musicals offer.' Following Dyer, Garland's performance in the film is itself camping rather than something to be camped.[22] **The Pirate** could also be seen to embody a 'queer' sensibility in Doty's terms because of its movement away from a constrictive heterosexuality and toward a liberating androgyny. The gay reading would first of all stress the 'queer' authorship of the score by Cole Porter and the 'queer' sensibility of Minnelli's *mise-en-scène* and arch, mocking direction of the actors' line and lyric readings. But the entire film deals with sexual issues of the most profound kind. I was always drawn to **The Pirate** for its spirit of liberation at the end; but the model proposed in the first edition, because it posited an ideal genderless reader constructed by the text, could not quite capture that this liberation was a movement toward if not bisexuality, then at least androgyny; that is to say, its vision of Utopia is a perfect world of freedom from the constraints of gender. Heterosexuality as masquerade, femininity as masquerade and masculinity as masquerade are important themes of **The Pirate**.

Hence the significance of the clown ending as opposed to the wedding motif which so structures the heterosexual reading of the musical. The fact that the wedding 'finale' occurs halfway through the film is significant in itself. In the wedding dress, having her portrait done, Garland is the model of stasis and femininity. But she is dressing for the wrong Pirate. The whole theme of the legendary masculine Pirate who is really the stodgy mayor questions not just the concepts of dream and masquerade but also of the construction of masculinity. As

Dyer points out, Kelly is highly eroticized in the film, especially in the hyper-phallic Pirate ballet.[23] But he is also coded as effeminate. A gay reading could access both Kelly's failure to be a 'pirate' (a fully phallic male) on the one hand; and his embodiment as a sexual object of Garland's gaze on the other. It is the gay icon, Serafin, the actor portrayed by Kelly, who becomes the true liberator of the woman by liberating her from the curse of femininity. The clown finale leads the couple beyond gender into an endless masquerade of genderless clowning, a transcendence of both masculinity and femininity through play and masquerade.

It has not been my intention to give a 'queer' reading of the musical genre; merely to suggest that such a reading can be grounded both historically and critically. The 'gay sensibility' that the figure of Garland evokes is by no means limited to one performer; it permeates the genre. Indeed this type of situated reading has implications for all the classic film genres that seem to rotate around heterosexual coupling; the screwball comedy (especially the figure of Cary Grant)[24] and the melodrama might also be subject to this kind of reception-oriented genre study. But, in following the vicissitudes of the musical film in the post-studio era, two historical audiences – the youth audience and the urban gay male subculture – clearly present themselves as actual historical precedents for readings of musical films; in the face of this evidence, we can no longer feel confident in speaking of an 'ideal' or 'model' audience for the musical or even of a 'dominant' or 'mass audience' reading of the genre.

Notes

1. *The American Film Musical* (Bloomington: Indiana University Press, 1987). All subsequent references to this work will be in the text.
2. In *Postmodern Genres*, ed. Marjorie Perloff (Norman: University of Oklahoma Press, 1989), p. 16.
3. *Hollywood Genres* (New York: Random House, 1981), p.24.
4. Thomas Doherty, *Teenagers and Teenpics: The Juvenilization of American Movies in the 1950s* (Boston: Unwin Hyman, 1988), pp. 3–10.
5. See Schatz, *Hollywood Genres* (New York: Random House, 1981), pp.36–42; and John G. Cawelti, 'Chinatown and Generic Transformation in Recent American Films' (1979), in Barry Grant (ed.), *Film Genre Reader* (Austin: University of Texas Press, 1986), pp. 183–201.
6. *The New Yorker*, 21 December 1981, p. 124.

7. Bertolt Brecht, 'The Modern Theater is the Epic Theater', in John Willett (ed.), *Brecht on Theater* (New York: Hill and Wang, 1964), pp. 37–8.

8. 'Shoot-Out at the Genre Corral: Problems in the "Evolution" of the Western', in *Film Genre Reader*, pp. 202–16.

9. Simon Frith, 'Video Pop: Picking Up the Pieces', in Simon Frith (ed.), *Facing the Music* (New York: Pantheon, 1988), pp. 97–8. Frith describes the marketing of the film and its successful soundtrack as an interwoven process; the film was conceived *so that* the soundtrack would succeed.

10. Noted for other musical films such as **The Turning Point** and, surprisingly, **Pennies from Heaven**. If nothing else, **Footloose** shows us that Dennis Potter is the true author of **Pennies**.

11. According to Brecht, 'The Modern Theater is the Epic Theater', p. 35: 'Our existing opera is a culinary opera. It was a means of pleasure long before it turned into merchandise.'

12. Maureen Madison, 'An Exploration of School Daze as a Musical', unpublished paper, 1990.

13. Linda Hutcheon, *The Politics of Postmodernism* (London: Routledge, 1989), p.11.

14. According to two recent scholary (and numerous informal) commentators on the subject. See Richard Dyer, *Heavenly Bodies: Film Stars and Society* (New York: St. Martin's Press, 1986), pp.141–95; and Janet Staiger, 'The Logic of Alternative Readings: A Star is Born' in *Interpreting Films: Studies in the Historical Reception of American Cinema* (Princeton: Princeton University Press, forthcoming).

15. Emily R. Coleman, *The Complete Judy Garland: The Ultimate Guide to Her Career in Films, Records, Concerts, Radio, and Television, 1935–1969* (New York: Harper & Row, 1990). Ethan Mordden, 'I Got a Song', *The New Yorker* (22 October 1990), p. 112.

16. Alexander Doty, 'Queer Culture Meets Auteurism', Paper presented at the Symposium on Cukor and Arzner, University of Pittsburgh, 15 October 1990.

17. Doty, 'Queer Culture Meets Auteurism'.

18. Christopher Finch, *Rainbow: The Stormy Life of Judy Garland* (New York: Ballantine Books, 1975), p. 207.

19. Dyer, *Heavenly Bodies*, p. 154.

20. Edward Baron Turk's 'Deriding the Voice of Jeanette MacDonald: Notes on Psychoanalysis and The American Film Musical', *Camera Obscura*, No. 25 (1991) represents just such a queer reading in both the senses I've just suggested.

21. 'Illicit Pleasures: Feminist Spectators and Personal Best', in Patricia Erens (ed.), *Issues in Feminist Film Criticism* (Bloomington: Indiana, 1990), pp. 192–3.

22. Dyer, *Heavenly Bodies*, p. 182.

23. Dyer, *Heavenly Bodies*, pp. 184–5.

24. For an already existing example of the type of work I'm suggesting, see Andrew Britton, *Cary Grant and the Comedy of Male Desire* (Newcastle-upon-Tyne: Tyneside Cinema, 1983).

Filmography

All That Jazz (Columbia 1970) d: Bob Fosse. Roy Scheider, Ann Reinking.

American in Paris, An (MGM 1951) d: Vincente Minnelli. Gene Kelly, Oscar Levant, Leslie Caron.

Anchors Aweigh (MGM 1945) d: George Sidney. Frank Sinatra, Gene Kelly.

Annie Get Your Gun (MGM 1950) d: George Sidney. Betty Hutton, Howard Keel.

Anything Goes (Paramount 1956) d: Robert Lewis. Bing Crosby, Donald O'Connor, Zizi Jeanmaire

Babes in Arms (MGM 1939) d: Busby Berkeley. Judy Garland, Mickey Rooney.

Babes on Broadway (MGM 1941) d: Busby Berkeley. Judy Garland, Mickey Rooney.

Band Wagon, The (MGM 1953) d: Vincente Minnelli. Fred Astaire, Jack Buchanan, Oscar Levant, Cyd Charisse.

Barkleys of Broadway, The (MGM 1949) d: Charles Walters. Fred Astaire, Ginger Rogers.

Belle of New York, The (MGM 1952) d: Charles Walters. Fred Astaire, Vera Ellen.

Bells are Ringing (MGM 1960) d: Vincente Minnelli. Judy Holliday, Dean Martin.

Blue Skies (Paramount 1946) d: Stuart Heisler. Fred Astaire, Bing Crosby.

Blues in the Night (Warner Bros 1941) d: Anatole Litvak. Priscilla Lane, Richard Whorf.

Born to Dance (MGM 1936) d: Roy del Ruth. Eleanor Powell, James Stewart.

Boy Friend, The (MGM/Russflix 1971) d: Ken Russell. Twiggy, Christopher Gable.

Brigadoon (MGM 1954) d: Vincente Minnelli. Gene Kelly, Cyd Charisse.

Broadway Melody (MGM 1929) d: Harry Beaumont. Charles King, Anita Paige.

Broadway Melody of 1936 (MGM 1936) d: Roy del Ruth. Jack Benny, Robert Taylor, Eleanor Powell.

Broadway Melody of 1940 (MGM 1939) d: Norman Taurog. Fred Astaire, Eleanor Powell.

Bye Bye Birdie (Columbia/Fred Kohlmar/George Sidney 1963) d: George Sidney. Janet Leigh, Dick Van Dyke.

Cabaret (ABC Pictures/Allied Artists (Cy Feuer) 1972) d: Bob Fosse. Liza Minnelli, Joel Grey, Michael York.

Cabin in the Sky (MGM 1943) d: Vincente Minnelli. Eddie 'Rochester' Anderson, Ethel Walters.

Carefree (RKO (Pandro S. Berman) 1938) d: Mark Sandrich. Fred Astaire, Ginger Rogers.

Centennial Summer (TCF (Otto Preminger) 1946) d: Otto Preminger. Jeanne Crain, Cornel Wilde.

Cheyenne Autumn (Warner Bros/Ford-Smith (Bernard Smith) 1964) d: John Ford. Richard Widmark, Carroll Baker.

Clockwork Orange, A (Warner Bros/Polaris (Bernard Williams) 1971) d: Stanley Kubrick. Malcolm McDowell, Michael Bates.

Country Girl, The (Paramount (William Perlberg) 1954) d: George Seton. Bing Crosby, Grace Kelly.

Cover Girl (Columbia (Arthur Schwarz) 1944) d: Charles Vidor. Rita Hayworth, Gene Kelly.

Daddy Longlegs (TCF (Samuel G. Engel) 1955) d: Jean Negulesco. Fred Astaire, Leslie Caron.

Dames (Warner Bros (Robert Lord) 1935) d: Ray Enright. Joan Blondell, Hugh Herbert.

Damsel in Distress, A (RKO (Pandro S. Berman) 1937) d: George Stevens. Fred Astaire, George Burns, Gracie Allen.

Dance, Girl, Dance (RKO (Erich Pommer) 1940) d: Dorothy Arzner. Maureen O'Hara, Louis Hayward, Lucille Ball.

Dancing Lady (MGM (David O. Selznick) 1933) d: Robert Z. Leonard. Joan Crawford, Clark Gable, Fred Astaire.

Dirty Dancing (Vestron 1987) d: Emile Ardolino. Jennifer Grey, Patrick Swayze.

Easter Parade (MGM (Arthur Freed) 1948) d: Charles Walters. Fred Astaire, Judy Garland.

Easy Go (alternative title: **Free and Easy**) (MGM 1930) d: Edward M. Sedgwick Jr. Buster Keaton.

Every Sunday (MGM 1936) d: Felix E. Feist. Deanna Durbin, Judy Garland.

Fame (MGM 1980) d: Alan Parker. Irene Cara, Lee Curreri.

Femme est une Femme, Une (Rome-Paris Films 1961) d: Jean-Luc Godard. Jean-Paul Belmondo, Anna Karina.

Finian's Rainbow (Warner–Seven Arts (Joseph Landon) 1968) d: Francis Ford Coppola. Fred Astaire, Petula Clark.

Flashdance (Paramount 1983) d: Adrian Lyne. Jennifer Beals, Michael Nouri.

Follow the Fleet (RKO (Pandro S. Berman) 1936) d: Mark Sandrich. Fred Astaire, Ginger Rogers.

Footlight Parade (Warner Bros (Robert Lord) 1933) d: Lloyd Bacon. James Cagney, Joan Blondell, Ruby Keeler, Dick Powell.

Footloose (Paramount 1984) d: Herbert Ross. Kevin Bacon, Lori Singer.

For Me and My Gal (MGM (Arthur Freed) 1942) d: Busby Berkeley. Judy Garland, Gene Kelly.

42nd Street (Warner Bros (Hal B. Wallis) 1933) d: Lloyd Bacon. Warner Baxter, Ruby Keeler, Bebe Daniels.

Funny Face (Paramount (Roger Edens) 1956) d: Stanley Donen. Fred Astaire, Audrey Hepburn.

Funny Girl (Columbia/Rastar (Ray Stark) 1968) d: William Wyler. Barbra Streisand, Omar Sharif.

Gigi (MGM (Arthur Freed) 1958) d: Vincente Minnelli. Leslie Caron, Louis Jourdan, Maurice Chevalier.

Girls, Les (MGM (Sol C. Siegel) 1957) d: George Cukor. Gene Kelly, Kay Kendall.

Give a Girl a Break (MGM (Jack Cummings) 1953) d: Stanley Donen. Marge and Gower Champion, Debbie Reynolds.

Glenn Miller Story, The (U-I (Aaron Rosenberg) 1954) d: Anthony Mann. James Stewart, June Allyson.

Go Into Your Dance (GB title: **Casino de Paree**) (Warner Bros (Sam Bischoff) 1935) d: Archie Mayo. Al Jolson, Ruby Keeler.

Gold Diggers of 1933 (Warner Bros (Robert Lord) 1933) d: Mervyn Le Roy. Ruby Keeler, Dick Powell, Joan Blondell.

Gold Diggers of 1935 (Warner Bros (Robert Lord) 1935) d: Busby Berkeley. Dick Powell, Adolphe Menjou.

Goldwyn Follies, The (Samuel Goldwyn 1938) d: George Marshall. Kenny Baker, Vera Zorina.

Great Waltz, The (MGM (Bernard Hyman) 1938) d: Julien Duvivier. Fernand Gravet, Luise Rainer.

Hairspray (New Line 1988) d: John Waters. Sonny Bono, Ruth Brown, Divine.

Harvey Girls, The (MGM (Arthur Freed) 1946) d: George Sidney. Judy Garland, Ray Bolger.

Has Anybody Seen My Gal (U-I (Ted Richmond) 1952) d: Douglas Sirk. Charles Coburn, Piper Laurie.

Hello, Frisco, Hello (TCF (Milton Sperling) 1943) d: Bruce Humberstone. Alice Faye, John Payne.

High Society (MGM (Sol C. Siegel) 1956) d: Charles Walters. Bing Crosby, Grace Kelly, Frank Sinatra.

High, Wide and Handsome (Paramount (Arthur Hornblow Jr) 1937) d: Rouben Mamoulian. Irene Dunne, Randolph Scott.

Holiday Inn (Paramount (Mark Sandrich) 1942) d: Mark Sandrich. Bing Crosby, Fred Astaire, Walter Abel.

I Could Go On Singing (UA/Barbican (Laurence Turman) 1963) d: Ronald Neame. Judy Garland, Dirk Bogarde.

I Dood It! (GB title: **By Hook or By Crook**) (MGM (Jack Cummings) 1943) d: Vincente Minnelli. Red Skelton, Eleanor Powell.

Inside Daisy Clover (Warner Bros/Pakula-Mulligan (Alan J. Pakula) 1965) d: Robert Mulligan. Natalie Wood, Robert Redford.

In the Good Old Summertime (MGM (Joe Pasternak) 1949) d: Robert Z. Leonard. Judy Garland, Van Johnson.

It Happened in Brooklyn (MGM 1947) d: Richard Whorf. Frank Sinatra, Jimmy Durante.

It's Always Fair Weather (MGM (Arthur Freed) 1955) d: Gene Kelly. Stanley Donen, Gene Kelly, Dan Dailey.

Jazz Singer, The (Warner Bros 1927) d: Alan Crosland. Al Jolson, May McAvoy.

Jolson Sings Again (Columbia (Sidney Buchman) 1949) d: Henry Levin. Larry Parks, Barbara Hale.

Jolson Story, The (Columbia (Sidney Skolsky) 1946) d: Alfred E. Green, Joseph H. Lewis. Larry Parks, William Demarest.

Kiss Me Kate (MGM (Jack Cummings) 1953) d: George Sidney. Howard Keel, Kathryn Grayson, Ann Miller.

Lady Be Good (MGM (Arthur Freed) 1941) d: Norman Z. McLeod. Eleanor Powell, Robert Young.

Lady Dances, The (alternative title: **The Merry Widow**) (MGM 1934) d: Ernst Lubitsch. Maurice Chevalier, Jeanette MacDonald.

Lady in the Dark (Paramount (Richard Blumenthal) 1944) d: Mitchell Leisen. Ginger Rogers, Warner Baxter.

Let's Dance (Paramount (Robert Fellows) 1950) d: Norman Z. McLeod. Fred Astaire, Betty Hutton.

Lili (MGM (Edwin H. Knopf) 1952) d: Charles Walters. Leslie Caron, Jean-Pierre Aumont.

Little Nellie Kelly (MGM 1940) d: Norman Taurog. Judy Garland, George Murphy.

Living in a Big Way (MGM 1947) d: Gregory La Cava. Gene Kelly, Marie McDonald.

Love Me Tonight (Paramount (Rouben Mamoulian) 1932) d: Rouben Mamoulian. Maurice Chevalier, Jeanette MacDonald.

Love Parade, The (Paramount (Ernst Lubitsch) 1929) d: Ernst Lubitsch. Maurice Chevalier, Jeanette MacDonald.

Lullaby of Broadway (Warner Bros (William Jacobs) 1951) d: David Butler. Doris Day, Billy de Wolfe.

Man Who Shot Liberty Valance, The (Paramount/John Ford (Willis Goldbeck) 1962) d: John Ford. James Stewart, John Wayne.

Married in Hollywood (Fox (William Fox) 1929) d: Marcel Silver. J. Harold Murray, Norma Terris.

Meet Me in St Louis (MGM (Arthur Freed) 1944) d: Vincente Minnelli. Judy Garland, Margaret O'Brien.

Monte Carlo (Paramount 1930) d: Ernst Lubitsch. Jack Buchanan, Jeanette MacDonald.

Murder at the Vanities (Paramount (E. Lloyd Sheldon) 1934) d: Mitchell Leisen. Jack Oakie, Victor McLaglen.

Music for Millions (MGM 1944) d: Henry Koster. Margaret O'Brien, June Allyson.

Music Man, The (Warner Bros (Morton da Costa) 1962) d: Morton da Costa. Robert Preston, Shirley Jones.

Nashville (Paramount/ABC (Robert Altman) 1975) d: Robert Altman. Geraldine Chapman, David Arkin.

Naughty Marietta (MGM (Hunt Stromberg) 1935) d: W. S. Van Dyke. Jeanette MacDonald, Nelson Eddy.

New Moon (MGM (Robert Z. Leonard) 1940) d: Robert Z. Leonard. Jeanette MacDonald, Nelson Eddy.

New York, New York (Chartoff-Winkler Productions (Irwin Winkler) 1977) d: Martin Scorsese. Liza Minnelli, Robert De Niro.

Ninotchka (MGM (Ernst Lubitsch) 1939) d: Ernst Lubitsch. Greta Garbo, Melvyn Douglas.

Oklahoma! (Rodgers and Hammerstein (Arthur Hornblow Jr) 1955) d: Fred Zinnemann. Gordon Macrae, Shirley Jones.

On a Clear Day You Can See Forever (Paramount (Howard Koch) 1970) d: Vincente Minnelli. Barbra Streisand, Yves Montand.

On an Island With You (MGM 1948) d: Richard Thorpe. Esther Williams, Peter Lawford.

On Moonlight Bay (Warner Bros (William Jacobs) 1951) d: Roy del Ruth. Doris Day, Gordon Macrae.

On the Town (MGM (Arthur Freed) 1949) d: Gene Kelly, Stanley Donen. Gene Kelly, Frank Sinatra.

One Hour With You (Paramount (Ernst Lubitsch) 1932) d: George Cukor, Ernst Lubitsch. Maurice Chevalier, Jeanette MacDonald.

One Hundred Men and a Girl (Universal (Joe Pasternak) 1937) d: Henry Koster. Deanna Durbin, Adolphe Menjou.

Pennies from Heaven (MGM 1982) d: Herbert Ross. Steve Martin, Bernadette Peters, Christopher Walken.

Philadelphia Story, The (MGM (Joseph L. Mankiewicz) 1940) d: George Cukor. Katharine Hepburn, Cary Grant, James Stewart.

Pirate, The (MGM (Arthur Freed) 1948) d: Vincente Minnelli. Gene Kelly, Judy Garland.

Presenting Lili Mars (MGM (Joe Pasternak) 1943) d: Norman Taurog. Judy Garland, Van Heflin.

Roberta (RKO (Pandro S. Berman) 1935) d: William A. Seiter. Irene Dunne, Fred Astaire, Ginger Rogers.

Rock 'n' Roll High School (New World 1979) d: Allan Arkush. P.J. Soles, Vincent Van Patten.

Royal Wedding (GB title: **Wedding Bells**) (MGM (Arthur Freed) 1951) d: Stanley Donen. Fred Astaire, Jane Powell.

Shall We Dance (RKO (Pandro S. Berman) 1937) d: Mark Sandrich. Fred Astaire, Ginger Rogers.

Shootist, The (Paramount/Frankovich-Self 1976) d: Don Siegel. John Wayne, Lauren Bacall.

Shop Around the Corner, The (MGM (Ernst Lubitsch) 1940) d: Ernst Lubitsch. James Stewart, Margaret Sullavan.

Show Girl in Hollywood (First National 1930) d: Mervyn Le Roy. Alice White, Jack Mulhall.

Showboat (Universal 1929) d: Harry Pollard. Laura La Plante, Joseph Schildkraut.

Showboat (Universal (Carl Laemmle Jr) 1936) d: James Whale. Irene Dunne, Allan Jones.

Showboat (MGM (Arthur Freed) 1951) d: George Sidney. Kathryn Grayson, Howard Keel.

Silk Stockings (MGM (Arthur Freed) 1957) d: Rouben Mamoulian. Fred Astaire, Cyd Charisse.

Singin' in the Rain (MGM (Arthur Freed) 1952) d: Gene Kelly, Stanley Donen. Gene Kelly, Donald O'Connor, Debbie Reynolds.

Small Town Girl (MGM (Joe Pasternak) 1953) d: Leslie Kardos. Jane Powell, Farley Granger.

Somebody Loves Me (Paramount/Perlberg-Seaton 1952) d: Irving Brecher. Betty Hutton, Ralph Meeker.

Sound of Music, The (TCF/Argyle (Robert Wise) 1965) d: Robert Wise. Julie Andrews, Christopher Plummer.

Star is Born, A (Warner Bros (Sidney Luft) 1954) d: George Cukor. Judy Garland, James Mason.

State Fair (TCF (William Perlberg) 1945) d: Walter Lang. Charles Winninger, Jeanne Crain.

Story of Vernon and Irene Castle, The (RKO (George Haight, Pandro S. Berman) 1939) d: H. C. Potter. Fred Astaire, Ginger Rogers.

Strike Up the Band (MGM (Arthur Freed) 1940) d: Busby Berkeley. Judy Garland, Mickey Rooney.

Summer Holiday (MGM (Arthur Freed) 1948) d: Rouben Mamoulian. Walter Huston, Mickey Rooney.

Summer Stock (GB title: **If You Feel Like Singing**) (MGM (Joe Pasternak) 1950) d: Charles Walters. Judy Garland, Gene Kelly.

Sweethearts (MGM (Hunt Stromberg) 1938) d: W. S. Van Dyke. Jeanette MacDonald, Nelson Eddy.

Swing Time (RKO (Pandro S. Berman) 1936) d: George Stevens. Fred Astaire, Ginger Rogers.

Take Me Out to the Ball Game (MGM (Arthur Freed) 1949) d: Gene Kelly, Stanley Donen. Gene Kelly, Frank Sinatra.

Talk of Hollywood, The (Prudence Pictures 1930) d: Mark Sandrich. Nat Carr, Fay Marbé.

That's Entertainment (MGM (Daniel Melnick, Jack Haley Jr) 1974) d: Jack Haley Jr. Fred Astaire, Gene Kelly.

That's Entertainment, Part Two (MGM (Saul Chaplin, Daniel Melnick) 1976) d: Gene Kelly. Fred Astaire, Gene Kelly.

This Time For Keeps (MGM (Joe Pasternak) 1947) d: Richard Thorpe. Esther Williams, Jimmy Durante.

Thousands Cheer (MGM (Joe Pasternak) 1943) d: George Sidney. Kathryn Grayson, Gene Kelly.

Till the Clouds Roll By (MGM (Arthur Freed) 1946) d: Richard Whorf. Robert Walker, Judy Garland.

Time, the Place and the Girl, The (Warner Bros (Alex Gottlieb) 1946) d: David Butler. Dennis Morgan, Jack Carson.

Top Hat (RKO (Pandro S. Berman) 1935) d: Mark Sandrich. Fred Astaire, Ginger Rogers.

Tout Va Bien (Godard/Gorin 1972) d: Jean-Luc Godard. Yves Montand, Jane Fonda.

Weekend (Comacio Lira Films, Films Copernic (France), Ascot Cineraïd (Rome) 1967) d: Jean-Luc Godard. Mireille Darc, Jean Yanne.

Wiz, The (Motown: for Universal 1978) d: Sidney Lumet. Diana Ross, Richard Pryor.

Wizard of Oz, The (MGM (Mervyn Le Roy) 1939) d: Victor Fleming. Judy Garland, Frank Morgan.

Woodstock (Warner Bros 1969) d: Mike Wadleigh.

Words and Music (MGM (Arthur Freed) 1948) d: Norman Taurog. Tom Drake, Mickey Rooney.

Xanadu (Universal 1980) d: Robert Greenwald. Olivia Newton-John, Gene Kelly.

Yolanda and the Thief (MGM (Arthur Freed) 1945) d: Vincente Minnelli. Fred Astaire, Lucille Bremer.

You'll Never Get Rich (Columbia (Sam Bischoff) 1941) d: Sidney Lanfield. Fred Astaire, Rita Hayworth.

Ziegfeld Follies (MGM (Arthur Freed) 1944 (released 1946) d: Vincente Minnelli. Fred Astaire, Lucille Ball.

Ziegfeld Girl (MGM (Pandro S. Berman) 1941) d: Robert Z. Leonard. James Stewart, Judy Garland.